Critiquing Personality Disorder

A Social Perspective

Other books you may be interested in:

Anti-racism in Social Work Practice
Edited by Angie Bartoli
ISBN 978-1-909330-13-9

Mental Health and the Criminal Justice System
By Ian Cummins
ISBN 978-1-910391-90-7

Modern Mental Health: Critical Perspectives on Psychiatric Practice
Edited by Steven Walker
ISBN 978-1-909330-53-5

Observing Children and Families: Beyond the Surface
By Gill Butler
ISBN 978-1-910391-62-4

Psychosocial and Relationship-Based Practice
By Claudia Megele
ISBN 978-1-909682-97-9

Social Media and Social Work Education
Edited by Joanne Westwood
ISBN 978-1-909682-57-3

Understanding Substance Use: Policy and Practice
By Elaine Arnull
ISBN 978-1-909330-93-1

What's Your Problem? Making Sense of Social Policy and the Policy Process
By Stuart Connor
ISBN 978-1-909330-49-8

Titles are also available in a range of electronic formats. To order please go to our website www.criticalpublishing.com or contact our distributor NBN International, 10 Thornbury Road, Plymouth PL6 7PP, telephone 01752 202301 or email orders@nbninternational.com

Critiquing Personality Disorder

Disorder

A Social Perspective

 Julia Warrener

First published in 2017 by Critical Publishing Ltd

British Library Cataloguing in Publication Data
A CIP record for this book is available from the British Library

ISBN: 978-1-909330-81-8

This book is also available in the following e-book formats:

MOBI ISBN: 978-1-909330-82-5
EPUB ISBN: 978-1-909330-83-2
Adobe e-book ISBN: 978-1-909330-84-9

Cover and text design by Greensplash Limited
Project Management by Out of House Publishing
Print managed and manufactured by Jellyfish Solutions

Critical Publishing
3 Connaught Road
St Albans AL3 5RX
www.criticalpublishing.com

Paper from responsible sources

For my father, who taught me how to question

Contents

Meet the author

Julia Warrener, PhD, is currently a Principal Lecturer at the University of Hertfordshire, employed as the Professional/Academic Lead for Social Work. Julia continues to teach social policy and social theory on the BSc and MSc Social Work programmes. She qualified as a social worker in 1993 and has worked extensively with adults with mental health problems since 1995. During this time she developed a particular interest in personality disorder. She is also a researcher and committed to service user involvement in research and practice. This book has evolved from qualitative research undertaken in the past seven years and explores the experiences and perspectives of service users and mental health social workers on personality disorder.

Foreword

This timely book focuses on the best way to understand and support people with personality disorder, who constitute the second largest category of people experiencing mental ill health in the UK and elsewhere.

Unlike most books in the field of mental health, it is aimed at social workers, service users and family members, as well as policy makers and researchers. Uniquely, this text is based on findings from the perspectives of both social workers and service users on personality disorder.

The book benefits from the author's long experience as a mental health social worker in a forensic setting, her PhD original research, as well as her experience as a social work and social policy educator.

It begins by highlighting the complex nature of personality disorder, the unsatisfactory diagnostic system attached to it, its multi-dimensional character, and the multidisciplinary divide. The external stigma attached to the label focused around the assumed danger to others by the person experiencing personality disorder, often ignoring the much higher potential risk to self, is recognised, as well as the impact of the internalised stigma in which the person perceives of her/himself as a failure, rejected by others, while wanting affirmation and acceptance. The high frequency of early traumatic experiences noted in the research on PD and in the life stories of service users to whom the diagnosis is attributed, which thus far has not been accepted as a key issue in the DSM diagnostic system, is singled out as an example of what needs to be taken into account not only in the diagnostic system but also in working with this group. By now we recognise that it is possible to experience post-traumatic growth, provided the right support is given to the person and their family.

All of the above leads the author to the adoption of the social perspective as the choice perspective, because it offers a more comprehensive approach, one that does not see the individual as a unit apart from their family or community, recognising our interdependency on each other. This social perspective relies on social work values and includes also the lessons from the new meaning of mental health recovery and interventions related to it, which are based on the strengths approach.

The author's original research investigating the views of both social workers and service users on what each wants from the other in the context of personality disorder is anchored in constructivist grounded theory and participatory research, a welcome departure from the usual positivist, questionnaire-led, research. The main findings illuminate the centrality of building a trusting, respectful, person-centred, relationship between service users and social workers as the base for their shared work which needs to include transparency and consistency, feedback, modelling, support for social and family networking and practical support. While not ignoring the need to avoid negative risks, the value of taking calculated positive risk is called for, alongside a trauma-informed relationship-based approach.

Thus the book provides readers with an alternative to the NPM (New Public Management) approach, one that can promote the wellbeing of both service users and social workers, and comes with evidence of how it enables safety and positive growth for people with personality disorder within the framework of social work values.

Written in an easily readable style, each chapter begins with critical questions, ending with a summary and followed by suggestions for further reading.

This book is highly commendable for social work practitioners, students at all levels, service users, managers, policy makers and researchers.

Prof. Shulamit Ramon

School of Health and Social Work, University of Hertfordshire

Professor Ramon is a qualified social worker and a chartered clinical psychologist, who has researched extensively mental health issues with service users as co-researchers. Her recent research projects and publications include: Women and Providers: Domestic Violence and Mental Health *(an EU project in five countries), and* Shared Decision Making for Psychiatric Medication Management *(a UK-based study, NIHR funded).*

1 Personality disorder: classifications, *myths* and risks

Critical questions

» *How is personality disorder understood?*

» *What questions surround it? What are their implications?*

» *Could psychiatric, psychological, service user and social perspectives be employed to better understand personality disorder?*

» *Does a relationship with traumatic experience underline the need for a multidimensional conceptualisation of personality disorder?*

Introduction

Personality disorder is a contested diagnosis. With a controversial history and more than one classification, as well as questions about responses to treatment, debate about its nature and antecedents predominates. Deliberation about the diagnosis has been evident since Schneider's (1958) revision of Pinel's (1801) original diagnosis of *'moral insanity'*. Pinel distinguished abnormal features of personality from traditional symptoms of mental illness whereas Schneider's *'psychopathic personality'* stressed continuity with mental illness. Dispute about whether personality disorder is distinct from both normal personality and mental illness (American Psychiatric Association [APA], 1994) has continued to this day, despite the lack of evidence to identify distinct categories of personality whether normal or disordered (Livesley, 2011). Furthermore, evidence suggests that personality disorder is often experienced with the more traditional forms of mental illness (Newton-Howes et al., 2010).

The diagnostic classifications reflect this debate and deliberation. Since its inclusion in the *Diagnostic and Statistical Manual*, personality disorder has been characterised as distinct from other forms of mental illness (APA, 1980). However, the World Health Organization characterises personality disorder within the same domain as the other forms of mental illness (WHO, 1992). These principal ways of classifying personality disorder are founded on completely different ideas about its nature and its relationship to normal personality and other forms of mental disorder. It is perhaps not surprising therefore that personality disorder is often poorly understood by mental health professionals (National Institute for Mental Health [NIMHE], 2003). Moreover, a number of perspectives offer alternative explanations of the diagnosis.

The psychiatric attention to classification, diagnosis and form (Jaspers, 1963) can be countered by explanations which prioritise broader dimensions of peoples' reality: the subjective, the social (Livesley, 1998; Tew, 2005) and, perhaps most importantly, the experience of distress (Castillo, 2003). A psychological perspective sees a relationship between maladaptive and adaptive personality and the extent of the former's impact on the self, relationships with others and society in general (Livesley, 1998; Ro et al., 2012). The social context and relationships within this, as both a consequence and a contributor to mental distress, are central to a social perspective. Here health and illness are seen as multifactorial, related to a person's social context, position and experience of power and powerlessness (Duggan, 2002; Plumb, 2005). A service user perspective offers a depth of detail about the experience of distress and most importantly offers us insight into the reasons as to why people might think, feel and behave as they do (Castillo, 2003). These different perspectives and explanations contribute a richness of information about personality disorder. However, by competing they can contribute to contested conceptualisations of mental disorder – to which questions about the efficacy of certain treatments, particularly in relation to personality disorder, only appear to add.

While clinical and research interest in treating the disorder has grown (Duggan et al., 2007), evidence for the efficacy of psychotropic medication remains ambiguous and unconvincing (Feuirno and Silk, 2011). No one drug is authorised for the treatment of personality disorder (NICE, 2009). Although some argue that the polymorphic nature of personality disorder means that different classes of drugs are often required (Stoffers et al., 2009), the National Institute for Clinical Excellence (NICE) (2009) states that drugs should not be used specifically for Borderline Personality Disorder (BPD) or for individual symptoms or behaviours. Moreover, drugs that are seen as '*good first line treatments*' (Stoffers et al., 2009, s 339) such as second-generation anti-psychotics should not be used in the medium to long term, and sedatives should only be used cautiously in a crisis (NICE, 2009). Questions about the use and efficacy of medication only serve to compound our difficulties in forming a coherent conceptualisation of the disorder, despite evidence that certain structured treatments can improve outcomes for certain diagnoses of personality disorder (Bateman and Fonagy, 2009).

However, a more coherent conceptualisation of the disorder, reflecting its multifactorial nature and drawing on these perspectives in equal measure, would help to minimise the questions which surround it and thereby facilitate greater understanding of person and diagnosis. This book sets out to consider this proposition. Within this it suggests that the recognition of traumatic experience is central to any reconceptualisation of personality disorder. It posits that this not only reflects the disorder's multifactorial nature but also the multidisciplinary context of modern mental health services. As a first step, this chapter sets out and critiques the different classifications in detail. The current and future classifications of the diagnosis (APA, 2013; WHO, 2012) are considered in the context of those which have gone before (APA, 1980, 1994; WHO, 1992). The aforementioned perspectives are then reviewed. The chapter suggests that no one explanation represents a *'gold standard'* (Trull, 2005, p 279) and that there are alternatives, which raise debate and can fashion personality disorder as a complex and contested diagnosis. The consequences of this for the stigma, stereotypes and myths surrounding both diagnosis and person are then considered. The chapter concludes by suggesting there is a need to, first, recognise the complementary character of these perspectives and, second, to hold each in equal measure to inform a more rounded conceptualisation of the disorder. It then goes on to underline the significance of associating personality disorders with traumatic experience, which calls for interventions that recognise individual courage, strengths, resilience and empathy. The chapter first offers a summary of the seminal literature on personality disorder to set the context for its later sections.

The seminal literature

The history of personality disorder appears riven with controversy and ambiguity. The works of Pinel (1801) and Prichard (1837) were crucial to the early identification of the diagnosis and the attempt to separate abnormal features of personality from traditional symptoms of mental illness (Prichard, 1837). However, the rise of the medical model, with its need to identify causal mechanisms rather than merely describe classifications or symptoms, led to a number of revisions of Prichard's concept of *'moral insanity'* (Prichard, 1837, cited in Tyrer, 2000, p 4). Schneider's (1958) influential revision of the psychopathic personality read: *'abnormal personalities who suffer through their personalities or through whose abnormalities society suffers'* (Schneider, 1958, cited in Tyrer, 2000, p 6). Schneider challenged earlier attempts to distinguish abnormal features of personality disorder from traditional symptoms of mental illness, stressing continuity with mental state disorders (Livesley, 2003). Whereas Cleckley (1982) argued that psychopathy was a distinct illness of the most profound deficit, Jaspers' work (1963) placed personality disorder on a continuum with mental state disorders rather than as a distinct nosological entity (Livesley, 2003). It is apparent therefore that current debates about personality disorder's categorical or dimensional nature are rooted in long-standing deliberations about whether the diagnosis is distinct from or continuous with the more traditional forms of mental illness.

Specific forms of personality disorder, ie BPD, have similarly been subject to debate and revision. Knight (1953), building on Stern's (1938) earlier work, defined a form which, he argued, was on the borderline with schizophrenia. Kernberg (1967) revised this early construct, defining BPD as a broad form of psychopathology characterised by primitive defences, identity diffusion and lapses in reality testing. Significantly, Grinker (1968) argued that BPD could be reliably assessed using discriminating criteria. While Grinker's work was influential in the inclusion of personality disorder and BPD in DSM III (APA, 1980), questions remained about its precise nature (Gunderson, 2009). Although revision can lead to positive change, it is apparent that the revisions of the general and specific classifications of personality disorder have raised many questions which continue to run like *'fault lines'* (Tyrer, 2000, p 6) through this area, which the most recent of classifications, it seems, has done little to assuage.

The recent and current classifications

For about two decades, personality disorder has been classified by the *Diagnostic and Statistical Manual IV* (APA, 1994) (DSM IV) and the *International Classification of Diseases 10* (ICD 10) (WHO, 1992). DSM is the standard classification system in the United States and the most widely used one in clinically orientated research elsewhere (Hebebrand and Buitelaar, 2011). It characterised personality disorder as distinctly different from other mental disorders. Personality disorders were accorded a secondary status to the more traditional forms of mental disorder; indeed, they were regarded as *modifers* which influence the more traditional forms of mental illness, such as anxiety and depression (APA, 1980). Classified separately on Axis II, personality disorder was defined in DSM IV as

> *An enduring pattern of inner experience and behaviour that deviates markedly from the expectations of the individual's culture, is pervasive and inflexible, has an onset in adolescence or early adulthood, is stable over time and leads to distress or impairment.*
>
> (APA, 1994, p 685)

DSM IV then defined three distinct clusters or types of personality disorder.

1. Cluster A, the odd and eccentric (including paranoid personality disorder, schizoid personality disorder and schizotypal personality disorder).

2. Cluster B, the dramatic, emotional or erratic (including anti-social personality disorder, BPD, histrionic personality disorder and narcissistic personality disorder).

3. Cluster C, the anxious or fearful (including avoidant personality disorder, dependent personality disorder and obsessive compulsive personality disorder).

In total, DSM IV identified ten different types or categories of persistent personality disorders (APA, 1994).

Although ICD 10 does not define personality disorder as distinct from other mental illnesses, it does define it as an ingrained and '*severe disturbance in the character logical condition and behavioural tendencies of the individual, usually involving several areas of the personality and nearly always associated with considerable and personal disruption*' (WHO, 1992, p 202). It does not separate the diagnosis into different clusters, but does identify nine different categories of personality disorder: (1) paranoid personality disorder; (2) schizoid; (3) dissociation; (4) emotionally unstable; (5) histrionic; (6) anankastic; (7) anxious; (8) avoidant; and (9) dependent. For 20 years personality disorder has therefore been classified on the one hand as a discrete type, distinct from other forms of mental illnesses, and on the other as within the same domain as mental illness (APA, 1994; WHO, 1992). One system identifies nine different types, the other ten. Both systems characterise the diagnosis as extensive and persistent, suggesting it is fixed and unchanging. However, viewing a social category as fixed and unchanging is the first step in seeing it as a natural kind, which can then be used to justify the existing social arrangements (Rothbart and Taylor, 1992; Yzerbyt et al., 1997). Perceiving a social category as a natural kind, comprising members who share a common essence, can encourage stereotypical assumptions and ultimately the construction of members as less than human, as the Other (Leyens et al., 2001).

It is argued that DSM V, published in May 2013 (APA, 2013), is '*of substantial importance for the revisions to be introduced in ICD-11*' (Hebebrand and Buitelaar, 2011, p 57; WHO, 2012). Standardising a common vision perhaps? However, it is argued that DSM V will encourage misdiagnosis, divert resources away from those most in need through the creation of millions of new patients and be extremely costly to the US economy (Frances, 2012). Such criticism from the Chair of the DSM IV Task Force indicates the extent of the controversy surrounding DSM V (Yasgur, 2012). DSM V's proposed revision of personality disorder was similarly controversial (Pilkonos et al., 2011). The ten different types of personality disorder were to be reduced to six (ibid.). However, feedback from a multilevel review indicated that DSM IV's ten categories were retained (ibid.; APA, 2013).

The general criteria for personality disorder as defined in DSM V is '*significant impairments in self (identity or self-direction) and interpersonal (empathy or intimacy) functioning*' (APA, 2013). For a diagnosis of personality disorder the person must experience significant and enduring difficulties in at least two of the following areas: cognition (distorted thinking patterns); affect (problematic emotional responses); interpersonal functioning (difficulties) and impulse control (either over-regulated or under-regulated). Impairment must be stable and consistent across time and situations and is not best understood as normative for the individual's development stage or socio-cultural environment. Nor must the impairment be related to the physiological effects of a substance or general medical condition (APA, 2012). In addition, each specific personality disorder will also have a separate list of asset criteria.

For a diagnosis of BPD, there must be significant impairments in personality functioning, either an '*impoverished*'/'*poorly developed*' identity or a lack of self-direction. There must also be impairments in interpersonal functioning, ie an inability to show empathy or engage in intimate relationships. BPD will be indicated by the presence of pathological personality traits, ie emotional liability, anxiousness, separation insecurity, hopelessness, impulsivity, risk taking and hostility. Impairment must again be enduring and consistent across time and situations, counter normative and cultural expectations and be unrelated to physiology or substance use.

DSM V was initially proposed as a bridge between categorical and dimensional approaches to personality disorder, with each specific diagnosis conceptualised as a disorder that can be assessed as both a discrete entity *and* comprising traits which can be measured on a severity scale (Pilkonos et al., 2011). However, is it possible to say that a category has a distinct boundary and also that it can be measured across a dimension? Possibly as a result of similar questions, the proposal to adopt a hybrid approach to personality disorder was not accepted and ultimately the Board of Trustees retained a categorical approach and the ten categories of personality disorder within DSM V (APA, 2013). However, the hybrid model has not been removed from the manual completely. It is retained in Chapter 3, to encourage research, as a methodology and mechanism for advancing future diagnostic and clinical practice. It is interesting to note that although DSM V abandoned the five axes of disorders, it has retained the specific categories of personality disorder, all of which raises the question of whether evidence exists to support such a retention of the categorical approach to personality disorder?

Research has failed to identify the distinct categories of personality disorder and has found that it is continuous with normal personality (Livesley, 2011). This would appear to explain why, in a survey of experts on personality disorder, 80 per cent were found to be in support of a dimensional approach to the diagnosis (Berstein et al., 2007). It is possible that a dimensional approach offers greater scope for assessing what personality does, how it 'serves to adapt individuals to their situations' (Ro et al., 2012, p 48) or not as the case may be. A dimensional approach allows for the role social and environmental factors can play in both managing maladaptive traits or indeed triggering distress and impairment (Widiger and Lowe, 2008). Given the lack of evidence for categorical approaches and, contrastingly, support for dimensional approaches, we are left with further questions about the efficacy of retaining a categorical approach in DSM V. It is quite possible that the confusion and complexity which has surrounded personality disorder since its inception will grow as DSM V is only likely to compound difficulties (Pilknonis et al., 2011). It may well add to the misunderstanding and stigma surrounding the diagnosis rather than challenge it (Livesley, 2010; NIMHE, 2003).

This section has suggested that differences and similarities across both systems for classifying personality disorder have contributed to a somewhat incoherent conception of the diagnosis. This is not to say that the tools for a more coherent conceptualisation of personality disorder do not exist. The value of each perspective is clear; it is more a question of how we use them. Perspectives and models which compete with one another, or are made to, can impair rather than enhance understanding. Polarised debates accentuate confusion especially if significant associations are omitted or overlooked. This chapter will now set out to critique the psychiatric, psychological, and social and service user perspectives on personality disorder and suggest that their more holistic use might further the understanding of this complex disorder, especially if the significance of traumatic experience is recognised.

The psychiatric and psychological perspectives on personality disorder

Diagnosis, as an explanatory framework for distress, is fundamental to psychiatry (Bracken and Thomas, 2005). Jaspers (1963) determined that form is universal and related to happenings within the individual and separate from content which is related to the social and cultural context. Causal explanations for universal phenomena can be discovered through technical idioms, neuroscience and a framework of psychopathology (APA, 2013; Bracken and Thomas, 2005; WHO, 1992).

Although both frameworks aim to standardise the classification of mental disorder, their increasingly narrow diagnostic criteria (Jablensky, 2005) can encourage heterogeneity and co-morbidity (Jablensky and Kendell, 2002), raising subsequent questions about the reliability of both frameworks (APA, 1994, 2012; Blackburn, 1988; Bowers, 2002; Rutter, 1987; WHO, 1992). Although a focus on form has encouraged research into personality disorder and its treatment, prioritising form over content can mean that we fail to account for the variety of ways in which individuals are positioned in social life (Parker et al., 1995). We are perhaps not encouraged to ask as much as we should, ie why the individual is 'exhibiting signs of acute distress' (Castillo, 2003, p 16). This suggests the value of drawing on supplementary perspectives in complementary ways, as it seems that no one perspective alone can explain personality disorder's complexity. This chapter will now review the psychological perspective on personality disorder. It will begin with a critique of the psychiatric classification before considering the value of a dimensional contribution to understanding the diagnosis (McCrae and Costa, 2003).

Although assessment and diagnosis are fundamental to psychiatry, with priority accorded to form over content, a psychological perspective seeks to explore and explain individual subjectivity and as such generally recognises the broader dimensions of a person's reality (Bracken and Thomas, 2005). For example, while psychology tends to explain personality disorder in terms of maladaptive personality traits, it suggests these explanations are insufficient alone, as environmental and social factors can mean that the person still develops functional self and interpersonal systems (Ro et al., 2012). It is the extent of personality dysfunction and its impact on the self-system, relationships with others and society in general which is important (Livesley, 1998). Consequently some have argued that the DSM in particular is inadequate for assessing the core dysfunction of personality disorder (Livesley et al., 1994).

As knowledge about personality disorder has developed so has the critique of the classification (Clark, 2009; Rutter, 1987). In the context of psychiatry's aim to standardise and homogenise the diagnosis, questions have been raised about whether the heterogeneity and co-morbidity of personality disorder is actually a consequence of narrow diagnostic criteria or a reflection of personality disorder's dynamic nature (Bateman and Fonagy, 2006)? The psychological perspective views personality disorder as a maladaptive variant of normal personality and as such suggests that this dynamic can be understood by the same set of traits which define normal personality (Ro et al., 2012). From this perspective personality and psychopathology are inherently related (Samuel and Widiger, 2008).

Allport (1938) argued that personality both *is* something and *does* something. Research has generally tended to concentrate more on the former rather than the latter (Trull, 2005). However, more recently attention has been focused on what personality does. If we consider what personality does, it follows that we must also consider its dysfunction (ibid.). While further research on the dysfunction of personality disorder is required, the Five Factor Model (FFM), derived from the five fundamental domains of personality – extraversion, agreeableness, conscientiousness, neuroticism and openness – is one of the principal dimensional models of personality disorder assessment (Ashton and Lee, 2001; Widiger, 2002). FFM assesses personality structure, traits including the maladaptive and associated social and occupational distress (Widiger and Costa, 2002). Assessing whether distress is at a clinically significant level is key (Widiger and Lowe, 2008), ie whether it impairs the person's relationship with self, others and wider society in general (Ro et al., 2012).

It is argued that the dimensional approach to personality disorder avoids the aforementioned limitations of the categorical classification (ibid.). However, psychologists acknowledge that the assessment of core personality disorder dysfunction is difficult and that the approach can appear cumbersome and less user friendly (Trull, 2005). If psychopathology is related to normal personality, it is not possible to characterise behaviour, thoughts and feelings as different in kind, only in degree. Without empirically devised cut-offs to identify significant trait elevations it becomes harder to define a person as with personality disorder (ibid.). Despite such limitations evidence suggests that a dimensional approach to personality disorder is favoured by clinicians (Bernstein et al., 2007). It appears that the assessment of personality deficits, strengths and the recognition of social and environmental factors in adaptive and maladaptive relationships can contribute to understanding the content of personality-related distress and rebalance psychiatry's attention to form. Such an approach might inform questions about the possible reasons for behaviour, and whether maladaptive traits, distress and impairment are a consequence of destructive social experience (Erikson, 1968).

The social and service user perspectives on personality disorder

This perspective considers the significance of the social, and relationships within this, as both an influence on and outcome of mental distress. Although defining a 'social model' might be difficult, some have articulated its relevance (Beresford, 2002), or at least the relevance of intersecting social perspectives (Tew, 2002, 2005), for understanding distress and mental disorder. Power differentials, both individual and structural, are highlighted with an emphasis on the internalisation of negative attributes of difference and the impact of this on personal agency and self-esteem. Analysis such as this can shed important light on personality-related distress; as silenced, a powerless person is not only at greater risk of abuse and victimisation, but is forced to struggle with society's expectations from a vulnerable position and with a more susceptible conception of self. Tew (2005) argues that this can force the person to establish personal distress patterns, ie combinations *'of rigid, destructive or ineffective feelings, thoughts and behaviours'* (p 81), which while possibly protective impact the person's relationship with self, others and society in general. Distress patterns resonate with research and literature outlining service users' perspectives on personality disorder, its complexity and apparent relationship to the social context (Castillo, 2003; Castillo et al., 2001; Fallon, 2003; Miller, 1994; Nehls, 1999; Stalker et al., 2005).

In addition to demonstrating its complexity and relationship to the social context, this literature reveals the intensity of the distress and how service users and mental health professionals can understand the diagnosis and the distress quite differently (Horn et al., 2007; Miller, 1994; Ramon et al., 2001; Stalker et al., 2005). For example, whereas personality disorder is classified as a heterogeneous entity (Bateman and Fonagy, 2004), Miller's (1994) research reveals striking similarities in service users' narratives about their experiences of personality disorder. Where individuals with BPD have been classified as experiencing identity disturbance and an impaired sense of self (APA, 1994), Miller (1994) found that participants expressed a core identity.

> *Common to all the patients was a view of themselves as estranged from others and inadequate in the face of perceived social standards. Rather than having an impaired sense of self, they seemed to have a sense of themselves as impaired.*
>
> (Miller, 1994, p 1216)

Reflecting Tew's (2005) *'hot potato'*, this is suggestive of the power of internalised, negative attributes of difference and the difficulty of struggling with these in the face of social expectations. Fallon (2003) too reports a commonality of experience, with all participants verbalising '*feelings of despair, hopelessness and depression*' (p 396). Participants' social interaction and behaviour were affected by '*strong paranoid ideas*' (Fallon, 2003, p 396) that could result in strategies to manage the sense of '*themselves as impaired*' (Miller, 1994, p 1217). Miller (1994) and Nehls (1999) suggest self-harm and suicidal behaviours as two such strategies, both constant features of service users' lives and consequences of extreme and chronic distress. Nehls (1999) argues that such behaviours are not attempts at manipulation but behaviours which they cannot control, as one participant suggests: '*Suicide attempts ... to me that's a sign of depression, and maybe they (providers) see it as being a manipulator ... I don't think mine have ever been manipulative. They have always been to me serious attempts*' (p 289). Such clarity about the relationship between chronic distress and self-harming behaviour underlines the importance of understanding the person's behaviour in its past and present context and the possible reasons for their distress.

This body of work (Castillo, 2003; Castillo et al., 2001; Fallon, 2003; Miller, 1994; Nehls, 1999; Stalker et al., 2005) also indicates how service users and mental health professionals understand the diagnosis differently. Stalker et al. (2005) found that although professional participants evidenced greater certainty about their understanding of the diagnosis, consensus among them was lacking. Although the majority named personality disorder as a psychiatric condition, others perceived it as a form of social deviance or rule-breaking. Interestingly, a minority of professional participants understood it as '*difficulty coping with day to day life, rather than the presence of a particular disorder*' (Stalker et al., 2005, p 364). Service users stressed the complex and varied nature of personality disorder and articulated different levels of understanding. Some service user participants reported that they had very little understanding of it, while others reported that it was a '*fixed condition, set in stone*' (Stalker et al., 2005), meaning that there was something '*fundamentally "wrong" with them as a person*' (p 363). These findings highlight the diagnosis's complexity and suggest the importance of understanding the reasons for the person's distress, particularly in the face of evidence which suggests a relationship with early traumatic experience. Over 80 per cent of participants in Castillo's (2003) study had experienced some form of trauma in childhood.

Each of these perspectives on personality disorder has value in its own right: the psychiatric for its attention to form and classification, the psychological for its consideration of how interpersonal systems, whether adaptive or not, are sustained. The attention to power, its use and impact, within the social model, has particular relevance for personality disorder, a relevance which is borne out in service user perspectives on the experience of living with the distress. However, an over-reliance on the form this distress takes, rather than its experience, can limit our understanding of a complex diagnosis. A balance between the form and content of personality-related distress is required. Our understanding is further limited when these perspectives are regarded competitively rather than used to facilitate a more rounded understanding of a complex disorder. A holistic approach to personality disorder is not beyond the scope of modern, multidisciplinary mental health services. However, the extent of stigma and discrimination which continues to envelope the diagnosis suggests that we are still far from a more coherent and generally accepted conceptualisation of the diagnosis. The next section considers some of the stigma, stereotypes and myths which surround personality disorder.

Stigma, stereotypes and myths

Too heavy a reliance on form and the classification of signs and symptoms can minimise our individuality as human beings and reduce the *person* to an essential essence. Essentialism has been found to be associated with stigma and the formation of stereotypes (Haslam et al, 2006; Yzerbyt et al., 2001). Goffman (1990) defined stigma as deeply discrediting labels which discriminate between the person's actual identity and their assumed identity. Crucially, evidence suggests that discrediting labels are more likely to be applied when there is an attribution of responsibility for the discrediting characteristic (Aviram et al., 2006). It is significant that discrediting labels are also more likely to be applied to those who are assumed to be violent or dangerous (Angermeyer and Matschinger, 2003; Aviram et al., 2006; Goffman, 1990).

In an important paper, Breeze and Repper (1998) found that the aggressive, violent, self-harming and generally disruptive behaviours associated with personality disorder encouraged professionals to perceive the person as *difficult*. Although such behaviours may be ways in which the person is trying to cope with their distress (Stalker et al., 2005), evidence suggests that these behaviours are frequently perceived as challenges to the professional's competence and control. The person is therefore more likely to be perceived as responsible rather than *ill*, trying to manipulate and wrestle control away from the professional (Breeze and Repper, 1998). Discrediting labels applied in the face of challenging behaviours serve only to distance the individual and impair the recognition of the person's distress and the reasons for it. A lack of attention to the reasons for why the person behaves as they do can contribute to myths and stereotypical responses to both diagnosis and the person. It appears that '*over simplified descriptions*' (Nehls, 1998, p 98) of people with personality disorder could be modified by greater knowledge of the content and experience of personality disorder, particularly given its association with early traumatic experience (Yen et al., 2002).

However, Hersch (2008) suggests that myths and stereotypes about personality disorder and BPD in particular can complicate effective recognition and treatment of the disorder. One myth suggested by Hersch is that '*BPD is a rarely seen condition*' (ibid., p 16), when in fact its prevalence in community settings is similar to that of schizophrenia at between 1 and 2 per cent (ibid.). Estimates of the prevalence of personality disorder are much higher. Personality disorder is prevalent in community, in patient and prison populations (Coid et al., 2006; Newton-Howes et al., 2010). Estimates in community samples vary between 5–12 per cent (Coid et al., 2006; Newton- Howes et al., 2010) and 10–13 per cent (NIMHE, 2003; Winship and Hardy, 2007). The estimates may vary, but it is found to be twice as prevalent as schizophrenia (WHO, 2012). This prevalence underlines the need for effective recognition and the support of distress. However, evidence suggests that recognition and support can be impaired by cultural assumptions and expectations, which again risk the effective recognition of personality disorder as it affects both men and women.

The diagnosis of certain personality disorders corresponds to stereotypical assumptions about what it means to be a man and a woman (Nehls, 1998). There is a clear pattern to the diagnosis of BPD in Western societies, where more women than men are diagnosed with BPD (Becker, 2008). While some dispute this gender weighting (Coid et al., 2006), the pattern suggests that the needs of both genders will be missed if professionals respond only to what they expect to find. Nehls (1998) suggests that expressions of dependency and/or demanding behaviour are viewed as natural in women and will be pathologised if they are deemed extreme. Similar expressions in men tend to be overlooked because men are not expected to behave in such ways. Furthermore, women are more likely to engage in help-seeking behaviours (Paris, 2008). Men are less likely to engage in help-seeking behaviours and are more likely to express their distress through substance misuse and offending behaviour (Paris, 2008). It is therefore not surprising that more men than women are diagnosed with anti-social personality disorder (Robins and Reiger, 1981). Discrepancies in the diagnostic pattern for BPD and ASPD add weight to the argument that personality disorder is little more than a codification of moral judgements (Pilgrim, 2001), which does not encourage effective recognition of, and support for, the person's distress.

Although violent behaviour can be perceived as a challenge to professional competence and control (Breeze and Repper, 1998), it is also associated with stigma and stigmatised responses in its own right (Angermeyer and Matschinger, 2003). Evidence suggests that the general public and mental health professionals correlate mental disorder with risk, violence and dangerousness (Nash, 2006). Perhaps unsurprisingly all of these features are clearly associated with personality disorder but appear founded on stereotypical myths and assumptions once again (Hare, 2003; Hersch, 2008; Markham, 2003; Pidd and Feigenbaum, 2007). Given that the evidence is contested, association between personality disorder, risk and violence should not be assumed (Corbett and Westwood, 2005; Pilgrim and Rogers, 2003). Many people with personality disorder face significant risk of suicide and/or accidental death given that many are *'prone to dangerous or impulsive behaviours or lead chaotic lifestyles'* (Pidd and Feigenbaum, 2007, p 8). Some of these behaviours may well be means by which the person is trying to cope (Stalker et al., 2005). Moreover, evidence suggests that those with mental disorder, including personality disorder, are more a risk to self than to others (Nash, 2006). It is also quite possible that correlations between personality disorder, risk, violence and danger are the relics of research methodology and reductionist forms of risk assessment which assume that the person is *'intrinsically dangerous due to their illness'* (Tew, 2002, p 144). Such assumptions only serve to reinforce the distance and stigma which surrounds personality disorder and prevents the effective recognition of and support for the person with the diagnosis. It is evident that recognition and support, including risk assessment and management, is informed by knowledge and understanding of the person, rather than distance and alienation (Watts and Morgan, 1994; Wright et al., 2007).

Stigmatising attitudes, within mental health services, can encourage distant, inert responses which foster alienation and escalate risk to self and possibly others (Watts and Morgan, 1994). Markham (2003) in a study of qualified mental nurses (RMN) and Health Care Assistants (HCA) found that RMNs perceived BPD as more dangerous than either depression or schizophrenia. RMNs were therefore less optimistic about positive change in BPD. Pessimism about positive change and an association with dangerousness meant that RMNs sought greater social distance from patients with BPD, undermining the possibility of effective recognition and support for the person's distress. Despite recent attempts to develop knowledge and understanding about personality disorder (DoH and Ministry of Justice, 2007), research continues to indicate how stigma persists (Latalova et al., 2015; Taylor,

2011). Mason et al. (2010) found that members of a key discipline continue to hold negative perceptions of people with personality disorder, especially with regard to the management of behaviour.

Greater balance between the form and content of personality-related distress is required if we are to challenge the stigmatising myths and assumptions which surround the diagnosis. When we assume that the person is responsible for their distress, is violent, dangerous or is attempting to undermine the professional's competence and control, we encourage distance (Wright et al., 2007) rather than effective recognition, treatment and empathy. Broader recognition of the relationship between personality disorder and early traumatic experience (Ball and Links, 2009) may not only stimulate empathy for the person as a human being, but also underline the importance of understanding their experience as an antidote to assuming that the person is responsible for their distress, will be difficult, violent and/or dangerous. Given this it is very unfortunate that traumatic experience, as an antecedent of personality disorder, is omitted from both current and future systems for classifying the disorder (APA, 2013; WHO, 1992). We know especially that personality disorder disrupts the person's sense of self, identity and interpersonal functioning (APA, 2012) and trauma disconnects the person from self, others and the world around (Herman, 1992).

Conclusion

We have suggested that personality disorder is a contested, poorly understood diagnosis. It has a controversial history; there is more than one classification and perspective with long-standing questions about its response to treatment. On the one hand, psychiatric, psychological, social and service user perspectives offer a depth of knowledge, explanation and research. On the other, competing perspectives, polarised debates and deliberation do not encourage a coherent conceptualisation of what is a complex disorder. However, this chapter has argued that a more rounded conceptualisation is possible, one which reflects the diagnosis's multifactorial nature that draws on the different perspectives, in equal measure, to inform a multidimensional conceptualisation of the diagnosis, its nature and consequences. The chapter suggests that this should not only be more than possible in multidisciplinary mental health services, but should be a prerequisite for this context. The chapter concludes by suggesting that personality disorder's association with traumatic experience should be central to any reconceived diagnosis. Consequently, the next chapter will define trauma and consider its impact on the person's connection with self, others and the world around. It will review the research evidence which supports a relationship between trauma and personality disorder. The chapter will also establish the value of a social perspective on personality disorder in enabling mental health professionals to empower the person's response to trauma and promote connections with self, others and the world around.

Summary points

- Personality disorder is a contested diagnosis and therefore effective recognition and understanding of this most disabling condition can be impaired.

- Competing perspectives and polarised debates can promote myths and stereotypes which encourage professional distance, alienation and risk.

- Balancing the form and experience of personality disorder might generate greater empathy and understanding, as antidotes to assumptions that the person is responsible for their distress, will be difficult, violent and/or dangerous.

- Traumatic experience is omitted from current and future classifications of personality disorder despite evidence to suggest that early traumatic experience is a factor in its development.

Taking it further

Bhugra, A and Ikkos, G (2011) *Reviewing Psychiatry's Contract with Society: Concepts, Controversies and Consequences*. Oxford: Oxford University Press.

Corcoran, J and Walsh, J (2006) *Clinical Assessment and Diagnosis in Social Work Practice*. New York: Oxford University Press.

Hinshaw, S (2007) *The Mark of Shame*. New York: Oxford University Press.

Out of the Fog. Information and Support for Those with a Family Member or Loved One Who Suffers from a Personality Disorder. Launched in 2007 the website is compiled by a team of people with years of experience of living with someone with personality disorder. Available from www.outofthe-fog.net

Widiger, T (2012). *The Oxford Handbook of Personality Disorders*. Oxford: Oxford University Press.

2 Personality disorder: related to trauma?

Critical questions

» *How is trauma defined and what are its consequences?*

» *Is personality disorder associated with traumatic experience?*

» *Can an awareness of trauma inform practice in the area of personality disorder?*

» *Is there a role for mental health social work?*

Introduction

Significant questions have been asked about whether personality disorder is indeed related to traumatic experience, particularly that sustained at an early age (Paris, 1998). The lack of longitudinal evidence for any relationship has been highlighted, as has a lack of specificity in that childhood trauma is not necessarily specific to personality disorder, and not all of those with a diagnosis of personality disorder have experienced childhood trauma (Graybar and Boutilier, 2002; Zanarini, 2000). However, we would argue that evidence suggests trauma, particularly in childhood, has a role to play in many people living with mental health problems, including personality disorder (Read et al., 2004). Such evidence is indicative of a need for mental health professionals to be more trauma-aware, in terms of its risk and impact and moreover, for how it might serve as a possible explanation for thoughts, feelings and behaviours. This appears particularly so given evidence that certain forms of trauma and abuse have been found to be increasing in some countries (Breckenridge and James, 2010).

Trauma, especially in early childhood, is known to impact on personality organisation and identity (Erikson, 1968), disconnecting the person not just from self but from others and the world around them (Herman, 1992). We suggest that greater recognition of trauma as both a possible contributor to distress and as, in part, an explanation for it, could promote more empathic professional practice to support resilience, strength and integrity. This is particularly needed in work with people with personality disorder, where we know that empathy for the person can often be lacking in mental health services, given evidence of their exclusion and construction as the other (NIMHE, 2003; Wright et al., 2007). Recognising the risk and impact of traumatic experience might help to undercut the stigma and exclusion which often surrounds personality disorder, as it is difficult not to feel empathy for those who have endured and survived damaging and disturbing social experiences. Moreover, empathy and support can help to repair the hurt (Winnicott, 1973). The relevance of social experience within this highlights a leading role for Mental Health Social Work (MHSW), within the wider multidisciplinary response, given social work's duty to understand how diversity characterises and shapes human existence (The College of Social Work [TCSW], 2012). Furthermore, social work and consequently MHSW has a role in challenging discrimination and inequality (TCSW, 2012).

Given the apparent relevance of trauma for understanding and working with people with personality disorder, this chapter will seek to define trauma and consider its impact on the person's relationships with self and others. It will consider the relevant research evidence associating personality disorder with traumatic experience. It will then summarise the different disciplinary models of intervention, including the 'social model' and suggest the latter's value in supporting a person's resilience and empowering connections or reconnections with self, others and the world around them. The chapter will suggest that trauma, as a feature of understanding, underlines the need for a multidimensional conceptualisation of personality disorder, which balances both the form and content of distress (Bracken and Thomas, 2004) and reflects modern multidisciplinary mental health services. The chapter will conclude with a proposal that MHSW has a particular role to play in any re-conceptualisation of personality disorder and in reshaping the response of mental health services to both person and diagnosis.

Trauma

Although the experience of trauma is distinct and unique to each person, it is an intrinsic part of everyday life. Although the risk of enduring a traumatic event might be differential (Breslau et al., 2004), all of us run the risk of experiencing at least one such event at some point in our lives. How we respond to these events will be unique to us as individuals. Some might discount or minimise the event, while some absorb the shock in an effort to 'move on', taking strength from adversity. The ability of some to 'move on' while others appear stuck or disassociated from the experience raises many important questions: was the trauma experienced as a single, devastating event or repeatedly, perhaps as a feature of relations, over time? Does the age at which the trauma is experienced impact on an individual's ability to recover? Can a person's social context contribute positively to resilience and recovery? These questions raise further issues about whether our current conceptualisation of trauma is broad enough to capture the range of experience and therefore maximise the potential for recovery and resilience (Gow, 2012).

DSM V (APA, 2013) defines trauma as the exposure to actual or threatened death, serious injury or sexual violation. The person or persons must experience this either directly or witness it in person or learn that an event has occurred to a close family member or friend or experience first-hand repeated or extreme exposure (ibid.). This definition is broader than those given earlier (APA, 1994). Events such as sexual assault have been included, as has the trauma experienced by first responders, such as paramedics, police officers and firefighters, from their exposure to repeated extreme events. The consequences of these experiences must cause significant disturbances in the person's social interactions, capacity to work or other areas of functioning. Distress and impairment should not be related to physiology, medication drugs or alcohol. The appreciation of trauma as that endured through repeated exposure to extreme events helps us to differentiate between what might be termed acute and chronic trauma.

Lee (2006) defines acute trauma as those traumatic accidents and single episodes of harm and/or injury which threaten the person's physical integrity or overwhelms their coping mechanisms (Van der Kolk, 1997). Chronic trauma emphasises damaging events or relationships repeated over time. Vulnerability to both acute and chronic trauma is heightened in childhood. In relation to the latter, Kris (1956) defined '*strain trauma*' as those day-to-day events which demean the child. This concept evolved with the work of Khan (1963) who argued that early childhood trauma can be cumulative, particularly when the child's dependent ego lacks the protective support of the mother, parent or caregiver. Bowlby (1973) argued that any events which seriously threaten the child's relationship and attachment to the mother, parent or caregiver should be defined as traumatic. Physical, emotional and sexual abuse can be perpetrated exceptionally or over time. The impact of chronic childhood trauma, however, appears particularly insidious as it can come to define or be '*typical of the relationship*' between the child and parent or caregiver (Kairys and Johnson, 2002, p 1).

Influential studies have revealed the consequences of childhood trauma, particularly in relation to the development of psychiatric disorders, lower social functioning and poorer defence mechanisms in adulthood (Massie and Szajnberg, 2008; Sroufe et al., 2005;). Indeed, Szajnberg and Goldenberg (2010) suggest that any experience which threatens the child's attachment may '*dampen a child's life course*' (p 39). We know that early trauma '*has long-term consequences for adaptive behaviour, proneness to psychiatric illness, expectable problems in motivation, cognitive development, memory, and information-processing systems*' (Wilson, 2006, p 90). Alderman (2008) notes, for example, how trauma can interfere with the brain's multiple memory systems, where the traumatic event can remain lodged within the amygdala, but can be lost from our hippocampus, our perception processing system. Consequently, when a trauma is triggered in later life the adult may experience a physical response, ie higher heart rate, muscle tension but be unable to translate this experience and the reasons for it into words. Given the range and severity of consequences we question whether our current conceptualisation (APA, 2013) is indeed broad enough to enable professionals, working with trauma survivors, to fully appreciate '*the reality of what happened to them or how they understood what happened*' (p 158). Greater awareness of the extent and implications of trauma and its relationship to all forms of psychiatric disorders, and especially personality disorder, may help us to get closer to this goal. Seminal literature can enhance our understanding of the relationship between early childhood trauma and its impact on adult personality.

Trauma, personality and consequences

Erikson (1968) suggested that early trauma, occurring before either identity or personality organisation is established, significantly affects adult personality. Erikson conceived that personality forms as a continuous, stage-like process, throughout the life course. He argued that early trauma impacts on this process of ontogenesis, particularly upon identity, ego strength and the person's ability to *master* threats, unusual stress and/or reactive memories (Wilson, 2006). Any attack on the ego strength, the *'guardian of meaningful experiences'* (Erikson, 1968, p 148), will compromise the person's ability to cope with the developing self and leads to a state of trauma ontogenesis or a post-traumatic state (ibid.). Impaired defence mechanisms cannot support our need for stability, consistency, or indeed our unity with the world (Celinski, 2012). Our social intelligence and capacity for empathy and our ability to *'understand other peoples' thoughts and reactions'* (ibid., p 17) become compromised, understandably leading to difficulties in our relationships with self and others. Or phrased another way, our self and interpersonal functioning can be significantly impaired over time and across situations (APA, 2013).

The risk to our physical integrity, social and interpersonal functioning and unity over time is associated with a greater risk of re-traumatisation (Briere and Hodges, 2010). As Lubit et al. (2003) suggest, trauma interferes with our adaptive mechanisms and can induce maladaptive coping mechanisms, which on the one hand can ensure survival, but on the other can increase the risk of re-traumatisation and be a source of trauma in themselves (Gow, 2012). However, although trauma can alienate the person from self, others and the world around them, it can frequently be overlooked, as Lubit et al. (2003) state:

> *Society will spend tens of thousands of dollars helping a child with a physical injury caused by violence, but it often does nothing to help with the emotional impact that can markedly disrupt the child's future well-being, work, success and citizenship.*
>
> (p 128)

This apparent failure to see the emotional, psychological and social consequences of trauma may relate to the primacy of Post-Traumatic Stress Disorder (PTSD) (APA, 2013) and to the challenges involved in working with trauma survivors themselves (Collins and Long, 2003). Kirmayer et al. (2007) argue that given the scale and variety of traumatic experience, PTSD (APA, 2013) can capture only a part of the experience. Moreover, classification and diagnosis limits the very essence of what gives meaning to our experiences: context and relationships. Indeed, Kirmayer (2005) argues that diagnosis *'decontextualizes and essentializes human problems, treating them as disorders that can be understood and treated with approaches that generalise across situations'* (p 462). Greater attention to the particularity of traumatic experience, as it relates to the personal and social context, would inform a more accurate and balanced understanding of the individual's emotional, psychological and social needs. Interestingly, Currier and Briere (2000) revealed how trauma awareness and orientation training enabled clinicians, in an emergency psychiatric centre, to better detect histories of both sexual and physical violence, which in turn informed their therapeutic intervention. However, attending to trauma survivors' experiences and needs is not without risk for mental health professionals themselves, particularly those engaging survivors in a therapeutic process (Collins and Long, 2003).

A range of negative consequences, for the worker, have been conceptualised: vicarious traumatisation (McCann and Pearlman, 1990); traumatic countertransference (Herman, 1992); burnout (Pines, 1993); compassion fatigue (Figley, 1995); and secondary traumatic stress (Munroe et al., 1995). Fundamentally, these concepts to a lesser or greater degree explicate how work with trauma survivors can both impact negatively on the psychological, cognitive and relational health of the worker and how care can be affected by the survivor and their traumatic material (Collins and Long, 2003). Failing to detect trauma therefore may be viewed as a legitimate, professional defence against being overwhelmed by the survivor and their traumatic material, protecting self from a range of negative consequences, both personal and professional. However, it must be said that not every professional working with trauma survivors experiences such negative consequences. Stamm (1999) identified that satisfaction in the helping process can encourage worker resilience, as does hardiness and good social support (King et al., 1998). Hardiness, they suggest, is characterised by feelings of control, commitment and change as a challenge. It is also quite possible that the capacity to reflect both in and on practice can protect the professional's sense of well-being (Wilson et al., 2011).

Evidence of the effect of trauma on the personality and the individual's ability to master threats, stress and reactive memories can effectively compromise the person's ability to cope with their developing self and relationships with others. This in turn heightens the risk of re-traumatisation. Despite the evident personal and social consequences, trauma can be overlooked as a possible explanation for distress. We suggest that the primacy of the current conceptualisation of trauma (APA, 2013) is a factor in this omission and can mean that experiences which sit outside of the classification for PTSD can be overlooked or defended against by mental health professionals. Moreover, the challenges involved in working with trauma survivors, particularly the risk of adverse consequences, can legitimate professional distance. Support and effective supervision are therefore critical to both professional resilience and the recognition of trauma as a possible reason for a person's distress. Awareness of trauma and support for the professional appears particularly relevant to personality disorder, given evidence of an association between early traumatic experience and the development of personality disorder as an adult.

Trauma and the classification of personality disorder

Evidence, indeed from within psychiatry, suggests a clear association between childhood traumatic experience and the development of symptoms associated with personality disorder (Lanius et al., 2010) or the diagnosis itself (Ball and Links, 2009; Briere and Hodges, 2010). However, as highlighted earlier, questions remain about whether childhood trauma can actually be defined as a cause of personality disorder (Paris, 1998). These questions centre on both the lack of longitudinal evidence and the lack of specificity (Graybar and Boutilier, 2002; Zanarini, 2000). Answers to such questions are difficult to obtain given the methodological, ethical and resource constraints on research proposing to consider the physical, emotional and/or sexual abuse of children by adults. This is not to say that longitudinal evidence of an association does not exist (Massie and Szajnberg, 2008; Sroufe et al., 2005), and just that it has not been possible to define childhood trauma as an aetiological cause of personality disorder. Consequently, the classification appears to stand with little recognition of the impact of early childhood trauma on adult, self and interpersonal functioning (APA, 2013). However, we would suggest that there is enough evidence of an association to warrant the attention of mental health professionals to the possibility that early, unresolved trauma might be a factor in a person's distress.

Interestingly, Bandelow et al. (2005) compared 66 patients with BPD with a control group and found significantly higher reports of childhood trauma among those with BPD. Parental attitudes were reported as significantly more unfavourable, with higher rates of family history of mental disorder and higher rates of premature birth. Indeed, intention is drawn to data which suggests that while only 6.1 per cent of BPD patients did not report childhood trauma, 61.5 per cent of the control group did not report childhood trauma as a factor. The authors conclude therefore that the 'aetiology of BPD is multifactorial and that familial psychiatric disorders and sexual abuse are contributing factors' (ibid., p 169). However, it is evident that the association is not just with BPD alone. In a two-part study, Berenbaum et al. (2008) found that childhood maltreatment and the experience of injury and life-threatening events were positively associated with neurodevelopmental disturbance and schizotypal symptoms, particularly in men.

Returning more specifically to an association with Child Sexual Abuse (CSA), defined by Briere and Conte as 'psychologically or physically forced sexual contact between a child (16 years and younger) and a person who is more than 5 years younger than the child' (1993, p 23), Zanarini (2000) estimated an association between childhood sexual abuse and BPD (APA, 2013) as between 40 and 70 per cent. Ogata et al. (1990) found significantly more reports of CSA, abuse by more than one person, and both sexual and physical abuse, from those patients with BPD than those with depression. Personality disorder is known for co-morbidity. In interviews with 235 outpatients with major depression, Zlotnick et al. (2001) found that those with a history of sexual abuse had higher rates of co-morbidity, particularly with BPD, PTSD, and also Axis 1 disorders. A history of sexual abuse was positively associated with lengthier episodes of depression (ibid.). Research indicates, moreover, a relationship between the severity of abuse and the severity of symptoms (Zanarini et al., 2002). Symptoms or consequences can include deliberate self-harm, suicidal thoughts and behaviours (Lee, 2006), acute vulnerability and severe emotional distress, including hateful thoughts and emotions that may be projected onto others.

Although we are not suggesting that early childhood trauma is the cause of personality disorder or that every adult survivor of child abuse will have a personality disorder, we do suggest that there is sufficient evidence of an association between early childhood trauma and the development of personality disorder in adulthood to warrant the attention of mental health professionals. However, recognition of this association is not without implication, as it would require a more empathic stance to those with personality disorder, who are more likely than not to have survived traumatic experience, somehow. A change in professional stance would be required. We know that people with personality disorder are frequently treated on the margins of mental services (NIMHE, 2003), perceived as difficult, overwhelming and a challenge to personal and professional esteem (Bowers, 2002; Hinshelwood, 1999). Despite laudable educational interventions (DoH and Ministry of Justice, 2007), we know that stigma towards this group persists (Taylor, 2011). Although working with trauma survivors brings many challenges for the professionals (McKim and Smith-Adcock, 2013), it is hard not to feel compassion for survivors of trauma of any kind. Whereas stigma can trigger defensive traits (Allport, 1938) and perhaps compound preexisting maladaptive behaviours, empathy and compassion can support strengths and resilience (Crisp and MacCave, 2007). Empathy and compassion for a person's survival can help us generate a more informed understanding of lived experience and the experience of distress. This calls perhaps for a more balanced approach to our understanding of the form and content of distress.

Balancing the form and content of distress

We know that thoughtful, empathic responses can inhibit anti-social behaviour in young people (Eisenberg et al., 2005), aggression towards others (Weisner and Silbereisen, 2003) and promote healthy personal development (Hoffman, 2001) and more effective outcomes (Forrester et al., 2008). However, a more empathic stance towards the person with personality disorder requires us to prioritise social experiences, both those that damage physically, psychologically and socially and those which promote individual strength and resilience (Scourfield et al., 2008). There is, therefore, an apparent need for greater balance in our appreciation of the form and content of mental illness (Bracken and Thomas, 2004).

Jaspers (1963) determined that the form a particular illness takes is universal and related to happenings within the individual. Form, signs and symptoms are therefore taken to be separate from the content or experience of distress, related to the social and cultural context. Universal signs and symptoms can be classified and moreover causal explanations can be discovered. Given that the psychiatric diagnostic model remains the principal model in mental health services (McWilliams, 2011), it is likely that form is prioritised over and above the experience of distress. Any such priority is endorsed by a policy context which, while lauding service user empowerment, fundamentally reaffirms a public safety agenda (DoH, 1983, amended 2007, 1990; 2005a, 2005b, 1999), and the prediction of course, outcome and response to treatment (Feinstein, 1972). However, given that distress is always embodied, en-cultured and temporal a call has been made for a rebalancing of the form and content of distress and for contextual issues to come '*centre stage*' (Bracken and Thomas, 2005, p 107). Greater attention to content and experience would sustain a more empathic response to the person with personality disorder because it would reaffirm the relevance of social experience, as both a contributor to and consequence of the person's distress.

The implications of recognising an association between early childhood trauma, personality disorder and relevance of social experience cannot be overestimated. However, if service user outcomes and experiences of mental health services are enhanced as a result of accepting personality disorder's multifactorial character, the investment appears fully justified. After all we have the tools at our disposal. While regional differences are evident, mental health services are increasingly integrated and multidisciplinary (DoH, 1990, 1998, 2006, 2008). The multidisciplinary context of modern mental health services lends itself to a reconfigured response, where the form and content of distress are balanced and orientated towards the multiple reasons for a person's distress and more fully reflective of the nature of human existence. A multidimensional conceptualisation of trauma and its consequences is central to any such reconfigured response to personality disorder.

Multidimensional conceptualisation and response

If trauma covers a large and ambiguous terrain (Kirmayer et al., 2007), no one discourse, be it medical, social or cultural, should lay a primary claim on explanation. Indeed, too heavy a reliance on the one perspective can distort and limit our lens of understanding. If we accept that individual trauma can emerge from, and impact on, a complex range of inter-related processes, ie the biological, the psychological and the social, our response should reflect these interrelationships. Each discourse or perspective has a role to play in generating a deeper, multifaceted understanding. Appreciating how the different factors combine to either accentuate the risk and extent of distress or to encourage personal strength and resilience appears essential. For example, our complex and, not necessarily linear memory systems, can trigger a physical response to danger at times, without our conscious knowledge. Although a permanent fear response may be lodged in our physical memory, we may not be able to put this experience into words (Alderman, 2008). The person experiences physical distress but simply cannot explain why.

Lasting memories of childhood trauma appear particularly toxic as they can condition negative emotional states, which can overwhelm adaptive mechanisms and consequently cause problems in identity, emotional control and interpersonal relationships (Briere and Hodges, 2010). Without recourse to explanation or social support, the person can develop psychological and behavioural defences which are maladaptive or coping mechanisms, which while protective in the first instance, ultimately heighten risk, including a risk of re-traumatisation (Kirmayer et al., 2007). The latter, incidentally, highlights the temporal nature of trauma and underlines the significance of understanding this experience in its 'personal, social, cultural, and political context' (ibid., p 466). While neurobiology suggests some commonality centred on the experience of fear, avoidance and stress response, it is the person's social and cultural context which makes the experience of trauma unique (Simon, 2012). We suggest that the experience of trauma survivors, the experts by experience, should ground a multidimensional conceptualisation and multidisciplinary response to trauma and by association personality disorder.

Having recognised how early childhood trauma can impact negatively on a person's neurodevelopment, vulnerability to stress, their long-term ability to regulate emotions and maintain coherent relationships with self and others (Lubit et al., 2003), the association with personality disorder cannot be overlooked (Battle et al., 2004). Given the detrimental consequences of trauma and evidence of its association with the diagnosis, we can deduce that a multidimensional conceptualisation of trauma is as relevant for understanding and responding to personality disorder as it is for understanding trauma itself. However, we are some way from recognising the significance of a multidimensional appreciation of trauma as a foundation for understanding personality disorder. While this may relate in part to the dispute over trauma as an aetiological factor for personality disorder (Graybar and Boutilier, 2002; Paris, 1998; Zanarini et al., 2002), the nature of the professions it seems can compromise a fully integrated and multifaceted conceptualisation.

A multifaceted lens with the person at the centre

Given the length and extent of professional training, both qualifying and post-qualifying, it is understandable that we, as professionals, tend to view any situation through our own particular disciplinary lens. As Kirmayer et al. (2007) suggest, we can remain within our own '*disciplinary boundaries*' (p 476) with our own ideas about what constitutes as evidence, and thresholds, for decisions. Psychiatrists need evidence to identify cause, psychologists to determine and understand how a person adapts to their broader reality, MHSWs to determine the impact of the social context as a contributor and consequence of distress. Consequently, professional approaches to evidence gathering range from those which need to control for context to those which seek to explore the individual's interpretation of their relationship with this very context (Tew, 2005). It is not surprising therefore that disciplinary discussions can be *difficult* (Kirmayer et al., 2007), with truly integrated conceptualisations a challenge.

However, if we are to take full advantage of the multidisciplinary context, particularly in relation to personality disorder, there is a need for professionals to accept our disciplinary differences while recognising our commonalities, particularly how human experience is central to all of our professional ventures. Such recognition may enable us to more fully appreciate the complementary nature of our different knowledge seams and integrate them more readily around what is at stake for the people we work with (Kleinman, 1999). Sharing power and working in partnership is, after all, at the heart of co-production, an enormous driver for change (Social Care Institute for Excellence [SCIE], 2013). The extent of stigma, argument and debate surrounding personality disorder suggests that a complementary and integrated professional response, which roots the experience of individuals and communities at its core, is very much required (Bowers, 2002; Tetley et al., 2012). This is important because as Kirmayer et al. (2007) suggest, '*There may be no one story that gets it right from biological, clinical, cultural and political perspectives*' (p 472).

The relationship between the diagnosis and its wider context is twofold. As suggested, there is a weight of evidence indicating personality disorder's multifactorial nature, with genetic, psychological and social determinants (Laulik et al., 2013). How the individual experiences and interacts with their environment, throughout the life course, but particularly in their early years, is crucial (Paris, 1996). Abusive experiences in early years are strongly associated with the development of personality disorder as an adult (Battle et al., 2004). Histories of dismissive, disorganised or preoccupied attachment patterns have been found to be associated with specific forms of personality disorder, such as schizoid personality disorder (Head et al., 1991), BPD (Reich and Zanarini, 2001) and antisocial personality disorder (Patterson et al., 1989). Given the weight of this evidence, a multidimensional conceptualisation of trauma is relevant to and reflective of the multidisciplinary context of modern mental health services. Moreover, the professional context calls for such a conceptualisation almost as much as the nature of the personality disorders. It could offer a foundation for a greater balance between the form and content of distress (Bracken and Thomas, 2004) and thereby would help to sustain a complementary and more effective disciplinary response, centred on the person's experience of distress and of life.

More effective responses are not just a matter for the person however; they have professional and public implications also. Personality Disorder was once thought to be unamenable to treatment (Sanislow and McGlashan, 1998). While it remains associated with poorer out-comes in the treatment of co-morbid conditions, for example, bi-polar disorder and co-morbid BPD (Swartz et al., 2005), there is, in general, greater therapeutic optimism for more positive treatment outcomes, especially from more longitudinal interventions (Bateman and Fonagy, 2000; Lamont and Brunero, 2009). McMain et al. (2013) found that those participants with BPD who were more able to identify and describe their emotions showed greater improve-ments in treatment outcomes, particularly in relation to symptom distress and interpersonal functioning. Interventions which offer opportunity to attach words to the experience, or phys-ical memory, may therefore help to affect positive change for the person, professional and organisation. Mental health professionals can consequently take greater optimism from their work in this area, which in turn might help to reduce personality disorder's demand on pub-lic health funds (Aviram et al., 2006; Rendu et al., 2002; Soteman et al., 2008). Moreover, professional optimism is clearly required at a time when service demand is increasing and service resources are falling (Shah, 2016).

Greater therapeutic optimism and the possibility of self-defined recovery underline our need to balance the form and content of personality-related distress and centre the person at the heart of our professional endeavours. Erikson (1968) offered hope by suggesting that the effects of early trauma were not necessarily permanent or pathological and that identity could be positively supported through a combination of resilience, strength and integrity. These qualities can help to enable 'trust in one-self and carefully selected others' (Wilson, 2006, p 103) through which the person may have opportunity for validation but also opportu-nity to challenge their more maladaptive survival strategies and therefore more constructive coping mechanisms. Not only does this underline the importance of relationships, but also the importance of particular relational skills and qualities which may encourage the trauma-tised person's faith in others. We would suggest therefore that there is a need to understand the consequences of traumatic experience in the context of the person's whole life, in order to support their recovery (Bracken, 2002).

It is apparent that one perspective alone cannot respond to the complexity of personality disorder. Our understanding has to reflect the diagnosis's multifaceted nature. Our response has to draw from each and every knowledge seam in complementary rather than competi-tive ways. Greater priority to the experience of distress would perhaps encourage critical reflection on why the person is behaving, thinking and/or feeling as they are. We may then have more opportunity to ask the *right* questions from which the person may begin to trans-late their experiences into words. Our understanding of person, experience of diagnosis, strengths and risks would be enriched; moreover, we might challenge the stigma of per-sonality disorder more effectively and in turn promote the person's strength, integrity and resilience. The next section will consider the social model in context before the chapter intro-duces the significance of MHSW to a better-informed response to personality disorder.

The social model in context

A social model sits with other, influential models, to offer explanations and platforms for intervention in mental disorder and distress. The psychiatric model enables an understand-ing of form to guide knowledge, possible outcomes and response to treatment (Feinstein,

1972). The psychological model offers a broader platform for intervention, as it assesses individual subjectivity in its broader context. A psychological approach involves '*the scientific study of basic psychological functions like perception, cognition, attention, emotion, motivation*' (Wittchen et al., 2014); it aims to address the '*why, when and how*' adaptive or normal functions can become dysfunctional (ibid.). A social perspective considers the significance of the social and relationships to the person's distress, as both a consequence and contributor to mental distress. While defining a '*social model*' is difficult, some have articulated its relevance (Beresford, 2002), or at least the relevance of intersecting social perspectives (Tew, 2005, 2002), for understanding distress and mental disorder, as we know that health and illness are multifactorial (Duggan, 2002), related to the person's social context, position and experience of power and powerlessness (Duggan, 2002; Plumb, 2005). The relevance of different perspectives offering alternative world views and methodologies for understanding and explaining mental disorder cannot be underestimated. However, the relevance of each contribution appears frequently undermined by the degree of competition between them. This appears particularly so in the area of personality disorder.

While research emerging from the psychiatric model has advanced understanding and interest in personality disorder, questions about heterogeneity, co-morbidity and the robustness of both psychiatric classifications remain (Bateman and Fonagy, 2006; Eaton et al., 2011; Ro et al., 2012). Moreover, it has been argued that neither classification can account for the experience of distress and the way power, position and context function in social life (Parker et al., 1995). A psychological perspective offers us a broader appreciation of a person's subjective reality, particularly in relation to environmental and social factors and how these can influence adaptive and maladaptive thoughts, feelings and behaviours. However, questions remain about the effectiveness of an approach which can assess the nature of maladaptive mechanisms, but appears limited in relation to establishing the degree of dysfunction (Trull, 2005). Despite the debate which surrounds these alternative platforms for intervention, they do complement one another in that they both offer explanations for personality deficits, strengths and the factors in adaptive and maladaptive relationships with self and others. Consequently, how they complement one another offers hope for a greater balance between the form and content of personality-related distress. It is perhaps more a question of how we utilise these differing explanations of personality disorder to fully realise their efficacy, rather than focus on any inherent limitations within the individual explanations themselves. Given the evidence of an association between personality disorder and destructive social experience, a social perspective might act to hold and support the focus of professionals on what is at stake for the person with personality disorder (Kleinman, 1999). With such a focus at the heart of our work we are more likely to be most effective. We would suggest that MHSW has knowledge and skills to first gain greater knowledge and understanding of service users' experience of personality disorder and second to help maintain the focus on the person and thereby promote a more effective response to their strengths, needs and risks.

MHSW and the social model

Although a social model of mental distress may not be theoretically cohesive, it enables us to both understand the social dimension, as both contributor and consequence of mental distress, and moreover how a person, experiencing some form of mental distress, may come to understand their position in society, particularly in relation to the powerful (Plumb, 2005). Its particular focus on how negative aspects of difference can be attributed to, and internalised by, the person, to foster stigma and social exclusion, appear particularly relevant for understanding the person with personality disorder. We know that stigma and exclusion surround people with personality disorder; we are also aware of how this can prevent the identification of needs and moreover hinder effective support and treatment (NIMHE, 2003; Tetley et al., 2012). Furthermore, through its focus on negative attributions of difference the model also helps us to explore the reasons as to why mental health professionals can construct the person with personality disorder as *difficult* (Breeze and Repper, 1998) to protect both their professional and personal esteem. However, the person, powerless and excluded, can be forced to struggle with society's expectations, from this vulnerable position, and with a more susceptible conception of self. The outcome quite possibly is the construction of a personal distress pattern (Tew, 2005).

A social perspective on personality disorder therefore can help us understand the contributors to personality-related distress; the experience of power and powerlessness, early traumatic and destructive social experiences and how these can come to form the basis of distress patterns through which the person attempts to balance their vulnerabilities with social expectations. However, a social perspective offers a means of underlining the importance of the professional relationship, as a mechanism for positive change, identifying strengths, to be supported through more prosocial interventions (Cherry, 2005; Trotter, 2004). The person might be defined as, essentially, a survivor of traumatic and destructive experience. Attention to their strengths of survival can support hope for rejuvenation (Winnicott, 1973) and recovery. Relational skills, founded on an attempt to understand the person's narrative and its consequences, together with broad social supports can help to initiate or restore a sense of connection or reconnection with self and others, which as Herman (1992) suggests, can be the antidote to trauma. Given the apparent value of a social perspective to mental distress, including that related to the personality, it might be fair to assume that social work and MHSW has made a significant contribution to this orientation.

However, despite some apparent connections, social work and MHSW specifically has appeared reluctant to support a social perspective (Tew, 2002). This reluctance might be explained by the contraction of the profession in mental health services (SCIE, 2008) and the priority accorded to its former statutory powers (Wilson and Daly, 2007). Its contracted or more diffused role may mean that MHSW has been reluctant to commit to the theoretical development of the social model for fear of further marginalisation or diffusion. However, the extension of statutory powers to other disciplines (DoH, 2007) means that MHSW now needs to re-emphasise its connections with its professional value base, the social model (Duggan, 2002), and make a theoretical contribution to its development. Through this MHSW may then be in a position to articulate its unique contribution to service users and multidisciplinary mental health services more clearly and to personality disorder more specifically.

Moreover, the Standards of Proficiency (SOPs) (Health and Care Professions Council [HCPC], 2012) call for this as they set out clear expectations about social workers' safe and effective practice from the beginning of their careers. These threshold standards, together with the Professional Capabilities Framework (PCF) (BASW, 2015) and Knowledge and Skills Statement (DoH, 2015a) demand that safe and effective social work practice is founded on the knowledge of social work theory and methods and that of the other disciplines to ensure evidence-informed responses to complex situations. Understanding the multidimensional nature of human existence and the impact of different experiences, discrimination and strengths to engage, build and maintain effective relationships with service users and carers is fundamental to the SOPs and consequently to safe and effective social work practice (HCPC, 2012). As such the SOPs, through their stress on knowledge, understanding, partnerships and the impact of social structures support a paradigm for MHSW practice in the area of personality disorder. They provide MHSW with a rationale for its contribution to the debate about personality disorder and the need to support people with the diagnosis more productively. MHSW's priority to context and the experience of distress connects with the social perspective to complement the psychiatric and psychological perspectives on personality disorder. As such, the priority towards the experience of distress may help to hold the focus of the multidisciplinary team on the person and what is at stake for them, balancing content with form and thereby encouraging a more effective multidisciplinary response to the person with personality disorder.

Conclusion

Although there may be an apparent lack of longitudinal evidence and a lack of specificity to verify trauma as an aetiological factor for personality disorder, we have suggested that there is sufficient evidence of an association for it to warrant greater attention from mental health professionals. Trauma can potentially serve as another possible explanation for the distressed person's thoughts, feelings and behaviours. The impact of traumatic experience, especially in the early years, on personality formulation, identity and self can be intense and overwhelming. Traumatic experience can heighten the risk of neurological harm, psychiatric disorders, lower social functioning and poorer defence mechanisms in adulthood. Trauma ontogenesis can impact on a person's social intelligence and capacity for empathy and consequently can effectively disconnect the person from self and others and moreover heighten the risk of re-traumatisation. Although its impact can be significant we have suggested that trauma and its consequences are frequently overlooked, by mental health professionals, as a possible reason for a distressed person's thoughts, feelings and emotions.

The propensity to overlook trauma and its association with personality disorder may be associated with the challenges of working with people who have survived trauma and those who are living with personality disorder. We know that such work can risk the psychological, cognitive and relational health of the worker. Alternatively, avoidance may also be associated with the primacy of PTSD as a model of understanding, which, as it classifies and abstracts behaviour from context, can limit the lens of understanding and exclude experiences which do not meet the diagnostic criteria. Consequently, if we are to capture the diversity of experience and its consequences, promoting hope and recovery, a broader, multidimensional conceptualisation of trauma can inform our understanding of and response to people with personality disorder. A multidimensional conceptualisation of trauma is as relevant for understanding personality disorder as it is for understanding trauma itself. Moreover, it suggests a need to re-conceptualise personality disorder by balancing the form and content of distress, utilising the different disciplinary knowledge seams in equal measure and firmly grounding the person and what is at stake for them at the heart of our professional endeavours.

However, personality disorder reconceived would have implications for mental health services and the practice of mental health professionals, including MHSWs. It calls for greater balance between the form and content of distress and moreover a more empathic stance on the part of mental health professionals towards people with personality disorder. If we are to support the strengths and resilience of people with personality disorder there is a need to prioritise the significance of social experience, as a contributor and consequence of personality-related distress, but also crucially as a source of rejuvenation and recovery. For no one discourse should lay a claim to the primacy of explanation; indeed, we have suggested that this can limit the lens of understanding. If trauma and personality disorder are multifactorial, our understanding and response should reflect the interrelationships between the biological, psychological and the social. However, there is a need to capture the uniqueness of human experience; therefore, we suggest that the experience of the experts, those with personality disorder, should be at the heart of a multidimensional conceptualisation and response to the person.

We have suggested that mental health professionals need to recognise their disciplinary commonalities and importantly how human experience is central to all of their endeavours. Disciplinary knowledge seams should be utilised in complementary rather than competitive ways. Rooting the person and their experience at the heart of both conceptualisation and response underlines the significance of social experience and the importance of opportunities to put this experience into words. A more empathic professional stance, founded on the importance of the person's experience, may just facilitate this and add to the growing therapeutic optimism surrounding personality disorder. The social model sits with others, to rationalise health, illness, disability and distress. Consequently, we have explanations for individual deficits, strengths, adaptive and maladaptive factors including the social, at our disposal. It is perhaps how we have used these explanations that is at issue. We have suggested that a social perspective on personality disorder, with its attention to context, power, powerlessness and experience, can help to hold the focus on what is at stake for the person at the centre of our professional endeavours. While MHSW's support of a social model of mental distress may have been more fully realised, we suggest that the profession's attention to context, experience, strengths, the relationship and critical reflection means that it has a contribution to make to understanding personality disorder and responding to the person so diagnosed.

Taking it further

Bracken, P (2002) *Trauma, Culture, Meaning and Philosophy*. London: Whurr Publications.

Bracken, P and Thomas, P (2006) *Post-psychiatry: Mental Health in a Postmodern World*. Oxford: Oxford University Press.

Castillo, H (2003) *Personality Disorder: Temperament or Trauma?* London: Jessica Kingsley.

Emergence; Changing Attitudes Building Lives. Causes of Personality Disorder. [online] Available at: www.emergenceplus.org.uk/what-is-personality-disorder/93-causes.html (accessed 13 April 2014).

Herman, J L (1992) *Trauma and Recovery*. New York: Basic Books.

3 Challenging the technical and rational: the importance of the social and relational

Critical questions

» *How is a rational and technical approach constituted?*

» *Is risk also socially situated?*

» *Has social work moved too far towards the rational and technical?*

» *What are the reciprocal merits of the social and the relational in practice with personality disorder?*

Introduction

We have recognised, to this point, the range of standpoints on personality disorder and the depth of knowledge they offer us. However, we have suggested that all too frequently wisdom and expertise are pitted in competitive rather than complementary ways, rendering personality disorder as contested, complex and poorly understood by the general public and mental health professionals alike. Service users encounter stigma and discrimination. Mental health professionals can feel deficient in both skills and confidence, which in turn can lead to avoidance, compounding the experience of distress, the sense of alienation and the complexities of the diagnosis. Stigma, both external and internal, in the form of self-stigma, endures despite increasing therapeutic optimism about the treatment of personality disorder. It is our contention that a balance between the content and form of distress will encourage a better understanding of personality disorder and generate greater empathy for the person who has invariably endured traumatic or destructive social experiences, probably from an early age. Too heavy a reliance on form can position the person as a mine from which causes and symptoms are deduced. Moreover, the identification of forms or categories of disorder suggest that the person has a '*fixed, underlying nature*' (Haslam et al., 2006, p 64), which risks attracting stereotypical and stigmatising responses rather than understanding and empathy.

According greater priority to the experience of personality disorder will encourage understanding and empathy for the person. We have suggested that MHSW has a particular contribution to make here, given the profession's commitment to understanding individual social experience in the context of wider oppressive and discriminatory social structures. However, social work is not immune from social pressures, the ideological, political and/or the economic. Indeed, social work reflects these very pressures, uncertainties and anxieties, ever more so because its attention to vulnerable individuals, groups and communities is more likely to be defined as failed or anti-citizens, seemingly incapable of making prudent and rational decisions (Rose, 1986). Social work occupies a liminal space, operating from contested if not oppositional poles spanning the private and the public, the subject and the object, which demands both knowledge and information (Parton, 2008). However, some have argued that in recent years social work has risked its attention to the social and the relational by embracing all too readily the objective ends rather than means and therefore information rather than knowledge and understanding (ibid.). Social work is in the eye of the storm (Webb, 2006) between the forces for the normative, rational, technical and the situated, responsive and substantive (Kemshall, 2010).

In its consideration of modern society with its careful preserve of safety, security and efficiency this chapter will analyse the implications of these drivers for both individuals and social work. The chapter will suggest that the demand for efficient systems and rational, responsible actors, at times of ever-increasing social and economic anxiety, fashion social work and determine negative constructions of those seemingly unable to meet the demands and expectations of their society. Consequently, this chapter will consider society's ever-increasing need to manage risk and social work's part within this. We will offer a critique of what are predominantly actuarial ideas and systems to suggest that as people are social beings, risk is an embedded and situated activity which cannot always be eliminated or reduced through the gathering and processing of information, calculation and management alone; but requires the technology of a relationship (Parton, 2008). The chapter will argue that the latter, founded on knowledge, empathy and understanding, can better inform every aspect of social work practice including MHSW practice with those with a diagnosis of personality disorder. Indeed, the chapter will highlight the particular merits of a relationship-based approach in the face of an apparent contradiction given that the person with personality disorder experiences '*significant impairments in self ... and interpersonal functioning*' (APA, 2013).

Modern complexities, uncertainties and rationalities

Social life is increasingly differentiated by opposites such as progress or failure, growth or recession, confidence or anxiety, the technical or the responsive. Seminal work indicates the former's dominance over the latter or at the very least an inherent tension between the formal and technically *rational* and the *subjective* in modern, capitalist societies (Touraine, 1995; Weber, 2012). Weber argued that the priority attached to teleological thought affords rational calculation, efficiency and controls a certain primacy in modern Western societies (ibid.), encasing our social worlds and trapping individuals within '*iron cages*' (Parsons, 1930) or '*shell as hard as steel*' (Baehr, 2001). Formal and technical rationalities combine to both identify problems and the means by which they can be resolved through reference to universally applied laws (Karlberg, 1980). Decisions can be made without '*regard to persons*' (ibid., p 1158). Progress endures, technology advances and efficiency becomes a necessary feature of our socially organic societies (Durkheim, 2013). However, the technical can come to supersede the humane when the only interest is to advance society's financial and technical state through information, rather than knowledge of our own humanity (Ellul, 1964). Certainly, the unremitting application of technology and rational '*laws of nature*' to our subjective, social worlds risks disconnection, from our will, as social subjects and our right '*to act and be recognised as an actor*' (Touraine, 1995, p 207).

Increasingly reliant on information, rather than knowledge, to calculate costs and benefits, the value of our social, creative and reflective capacities are denied, in favour of responsible, prudent, rational thoughts, decision making and behaviours (Kemshall, 2010). This is not to suggest that the role and function of the rational actor is without merit, but more that without reciprocal attention to the complexities of social life and equal value for our abilities to interact with, navigate and adapt to dynamic situations, we risk losing sight of the importance of ourselves as social actors engaged in face-to-face relationships for trust and security (Giddens, 2013). Over-reliance on formal, technical rationalities can not only dehumanise but fatefully alienate those deemed as irresponsible, irrational and lacking prudence, particularly at fateful moments (Giddens, 2013). Such moments are defined as landmark instants when factors combine to impinge on the lives of individuals and/or communities, particularly in relation to risk. Giddens suggests it is at these very moments that experts are commonly called to assess the risk of specific consequences, but it is the individual or community who has to live with the risk and its consequences, in dynamic social environments (ibid.). It is important therefore for us to recognise the interdependency of our rational and social selves and moreover accord equal weight to both, as while technical expertise may help us to identify risk, it is our creative, reflective and social capacities that enable us to live with it in complex, late modern society. However, evidence suggests that we can dismiss that which is *risky*, different or seemingly irrational all too readily, or at the very least engage superficially, without exploring the reasons for it, the reasons as to why people think, feel and behave as they do (Wilson et al., 2011).

As Western societies have advanced, we are seemingly less concerned with understanding subjects' experience of modern life, with its opportunities, shocks and uncertainties and are more concerned with managing and regulating risk and security (Webb, 2006). Yet, as Simmel suggests primacy of the rational and the objective risks alienation and indifference to everything subjective (cited in Frisby, 1992). Yet it is the knowledge of the subject, both self and others, coupled with a capacity for reflection which helps us to understand and make sense of risk within very complex lives, both our own and in interaction with each other, risks in the lives of others (Webb, 2006). This is so because risk is socially contingent and situated within a multiplicity of factors, including resources and political commitments, making it rife with meaning (Denscombe, 2003). For example, the self-harming behaviours associated with personality disorder are often perceived as risking fatal injury, manipulative and/or attention seeking. Taken from the person's perspective, however, self-harm is frequently a safety valve, a means of releasing intense emotional distress and therefore a mechanism for survival (Castillo, 2003). Unfortunately, the more *rational* and reductionist explanations of behaviour can engulf and overpower the subject's explanation, the expert in experience, which leaves us with only a partial explanation of why someone might engage in self-harm.

Knowledge of the subject and of their social situation is vital to understanding the problems and risks associated with life in complex modern societies. Attention to the rational and objective alone risks partial understandings and the alienation of those deemed as less than rational, responsible or prudent. Not only does this cement negative constructions of the Other (Wright et al., 2007), but alienated distance impairs knowledge and the understanding of the person and consequently compounds risk over the longer term. Knowledge of the subject, of their experience and perspective appears essential to a better-informed understanding of personality disorder, particularly as it is so associated with complexity, risk, dangerousness and exclusion (NIMHE, 2003). It is regrettable therefore that mental health policy, including that relevant to personality disorder, has looked to assuage public concern about the risks associated with mental health problems, without fully appreciating the nature of those risks and how we might best work with them, possibly because mental health policy tends to support normative assumptions about mental disorder and, moreover, relies on a supposition that both service users and practitioners are rational actors alone (Kemshall, 2010).

The policy context

We suggested in Chapter 1 that mental health professionals and the general public connect mental disorder with risk, violence and dangerousness (Nash, 2006). Interestingly, while recent evidence indicates positive change in public attitudes to mental illness in the UK, an association with violence endures (MIND, 2014). Time for Change has once again surveyed a sample of the UK population, asking 1,714 adults to rate how much they agreed or disagreed with a number of statements about mental illness. Results suggest that we, the general public, are now more willing to have a friend, to work with or live near someone with mental illness. However, while respondents used the descriptor '*Is prone to violence*' less in 2013, data from the previous decade reveals a steady correlation between mental illness and violence. Twenty-nine per cent of the sample, in 2003, described someone with mental illness as being '*prone to violence*'. This rose to 36 per cent in 2008, peaked at 37 per cent in 2011 before falling to 32 per cent in 2013 (ibid.). The public's correlation between violence and mental illness translates into a political commitment to protect both *patients* and public, but particularly the latter, from harm (Munro, 2004). Public inquiry, policy and practice can be seen therefore as a means of investigating and reducing the problem of risk and actual violence, so as to dampen and dissemble '*public disquiet about scandal or a disaster*' (Blom-Cooper, 1996, p 57). Unfortunately, politicians, media and public can overestimate the risk of violence and our ability, as professionals, to predict it (Eldergill, 2002). Any correlation between violence and personality disorder requires careful consideration and should not simply be assumed (Corbett and Westwood, 2005). Nevertheless, policy has tended to reflect an assumption that illness equates with dangerousness without regard for its subjective meaning or the detail of the risk in question.

Attention to the personal and the individual has therefore been undercut by a policy context which has prioritised public safety, control and service rationing (DoH, 1983, 1990, 1999a, 1999b, 2005a, 2005b, amended 2007). Individuals' vulnerability does require compulsory treatment (DoH, 1983, amended 2007) and safeguarding (Office of the Public Guardian, 2013) at times, but current priorities limit attempts to understand the reasons for distress and the probability of its connection to the social situation. The primacy of control and management over understanding and knowledge needs to be considered alongside pervasive neo-liberal obligations to '*roll back*' *and* '*roll out*' the state (Newman, 2011, p 93). New Labour, in particular, aimed to establish a new contract between citizen and state based on the acquisition of rights with responsibility to secure economic competitiveness and safe and responsible communities (Jordon, 2001). Modernisation through the Third Way (Giddens, 1999) had significant implications for public services, as it extended the marketisation implemented by the previous Conservative governments (DoH, 1990). In the context of progressive deinstitutionalisation (Campbell and Davidson, 2012), mental health services have increasingly prioritised public safety (Ryan and Morgan, 2004), surveillance and control over and above engaging the person in a therapeutic relationship to promote recovery, meaning and purpose (Ryan et al., 2012). While community Treatment Orders are seemingly rarely used with people with personality disorder (Malik and Hussain, 2009), their effectiveness, as a means of delivering greater safety and control, is questionable given evidence which suggests that such interventions can actually have the reverse effect, making the person more reluctant to engage and therefore exacerbating, rather than reducing, risk to self and others (Ryan and Morgan, 2004).

Reform of the legislative provisions for personality disorder (DoH, 1983) was initiated in this ideological and organisational context. This is not to say that reform in relation to personality disorder was not required. It was required, particularly given the stipulation that any application for detention had to consider treatability, ie whether admission was likely to alleviate or prevent deterioration in the condition (DoH, 1983). This, together with the omission of personality disorder as a separate definition of disorder (DoH, 1983), meant that there was always had limited access to treatment (Lewis and Appleby, 1988). However, it was proposed that those with a Dangerous and Severe Personality Disorder (DSPD) could be detained indefinitely to protect the public. Any such detention could be based on the risk of *likely*, rather than *actual*, harm (DoH, 1999b, 2000). While the government recognised that protective custody would infringe individual rights (Rozenberg, 2001), the rights of the individual had to be balanced against the rights of the public at the risk of future harm. These proposals, although eventually dropped (DoH, 2004b), reinforced the risk, dangerousness and un-treatability of personality disorder (Castillo, 2010), further establishing the need for control and exacerbating the stigma and exclusion surrounding the personality disorder. Moreover, it contradicted specific and radical policy guidance to implement the National Services Framework for Mental Health (NSF) (DoH, 1999c) for personality disorder and ultimately challenged its exclusion in mental health services and wider society.

Personality Disorder: No Longer a Diagnosis of Exclusion (NIMHE, 2003) built on an earlier scoping study identifying significant weaknesses in service arrangements and profound antipathy of staff towards people with personality disorder (Duggan, 2001). Its objectives were threefold: to assist those with personality disorder to access services; to ensure that offenders receive appropriate forensic care; and to ensure that professionals receive appropriate training and continuing professional development opportunities in relation to personality disorder (NIMHE, 2003). Although the *management* (NIMHE, 2003, p 6) of personality disorder remained a priority, this policy sought to develop good practice through specialist multidisciplinary teams and specialist day patient services and moreover to encourage optimism about the effectiveness of therapeutic interventions (Bateman and Tyrer, 2002). The inclusion of service users' perspectives was important to the achievement of these objectives (NIMHE, 2003). Crucially, service users suggested that there is a need for a '*shared experience between patient and professional'* (ibid., p 21) and for the professional to be in touch with the person's distress but not overwhelmed by it. In this way NIMHE (2003) valued the subjective content of distress, providing an important counterbalance to those more rational and reductionist explanations and responses to the diagnosis. The document's support for the person's perspective and experience makes the decision to implement the policy as guidance, rather than as strategy, doubly disappointing, as it seems its success was limited from the outset (NIMHE, 2003).

Such specific attention to personality disorder is missing in more recent policy, which asserts a more general need to close the equality gap and improve access to mental health services and therapies (DoH, 2009, 2010). However, these objectives are set in an increasingly managerial and privatised economy of care (Pemberton, 2012; DoH, 2012) and at a time of severe fiscal and service retrenchment (Taylor-Gooby, 2011). Empowerment through an increase in market *choice*, rather than through active citizenship (Postle and Beresford, 2007), continues the top–down consumerist, neo-liberal premise of contemporary policy (Beresford and Croft, 2001) and acts to prevent the acquisition of political, social and civil rights (Marshall, 1987). Empowerment approaches that assert the importance of choice without addressing structural inequalities are conceptually problematic, especially at a time of economic crisis, fiscal restraint and service retrenchment (Taylor-Gooby, 2012).

The government's national strategy for mental health (DoH, 2010, 2014) needs therefore to be viewed in the wider context of fiscal restraint and structural inequality (Institute for Fiscal Studies, 2010). While the strategy prioritises early intervention, service integration, personalisation and recovery, adjoined with the Care Act's commitment to prevention, the promotion of well-being, advocacy and a national threshold on eligibility (DoH, 2014), it is hard to see how these objectives will be realised in the current or foreseeable future. Evidence suggests that while mental health trusts are currently managing an 8.25 per cent cut in real terms, referral rates have increased by 20 per cent (BBC, 2015). A strategy that emphasises restraint, control and commissioning (DoH, 2010) over and above process and resourcing is unlikely to achieve its objective of ultimately reducing risk. We are critical of policy merely as a means to identify and resolve the *problem* of mental illness, its risks and dangers that need to be controlled. If policy objectives do not allow, or are not offset, with empathy for the person's social experience, knowledge and understanding of the reasons why people think, feel and behave as they do risk, stigma and exclusion will not be confronted. Our rational and social selves need to be understood as interdependent and in balance. The subjective experience of distress, the content or experience of personality disorder can and should inform our understanding and approach to both person and diagnosis. We might anticipate that social work has a role to play here. However, evidence suggests that social work has been heavily influenced by the technically rational, risk, the neo-liberal attention to the market and consequently has fashioned more legal and administrative responses (Wilson et al., 2011).

Social work: technical and rational

As a global profession social work is committed to social change, development, social cohesion, empowerment and the liberation of individuals, groups and communities. Founded on principles of social justice, human rights, collective responsibility and respect for diversities social workers engage with people to help them address challenges within their lives to enhance their well-being (International Federation of Social Work [IFSW], 2014). We saw in Chapter 2 how these commitments, principles and aims translate, in the UK context, into codes, standards and frameworks for practice (BASW, 2012; HCPC, 2012; TCSW, 2012). All reflect the profession's duality in that social work and social workers are expected, through the maintenance of a professional relationship based on respect, privacy, reliability and confidentiality (BASW, 2012), to establish and maintain the trust and confidence of those who use social work services (TCSW, 2012). In this way practice can promote social justice and address discrimination, disadvantage and oppression (HCPC, 2012). However, social workers also have to safeguard and address practices which present risks to self and others (ibid.). We would suggest that, taken together, these expectations reflect the profession's social and rational boundaries and social workers' identities as both social and rational actors (Kemshall, 2010). However, interestingly, social work's consideration of risk should uphold personal autonomy and should not prevent the taking of reasonable risks (BASW, 2012; TCSW, 2012). Here risk is connoted more positively it would seem as a necessary counterbalance to modernity's intention to avoid, eliminate or at the very least regulate risk (Webb, 2006). Social work's commitment to the *'right to fail'* (Ramon, 2005, p 191) should not be forgotten as a mechanism for learning, developing and respecting both individual and collective strengths. Practice, skills and proficiencies should balance needs *with* strengths and safety *with* positive risk taking (NIMHE, 2004). However, evidence suggests that in recent years, social work's technical rationality has overwhelmed the more situated and subjective, to ensure that practitioners and employers perceive risk more negatively and are therefore more fearful of positive risk taking in any form (Ramon, 2005). Indeed, some have argued that late modernity's concern for security and regulation *'has re-oriented social work practice towards managing and securing against risk as opposed to genuine attempts to respond meaningfully to need'* (Stanford, 2010, p 1065).

Beck (1992) argued that risk was a product of modernisation. The totality of risk means that we are never fully aware, which in turn leads us to feel ever more insecure, *'at risk'* and sceptical of *'expert knowledge'* (Webb, 2006). The growth of individualisation, the demise of conventional social ties and of our faith in the political realm renders the traditional institutions of accountability and control inadequate. New forms of regulation are required, if we are to counter all pervasive risk. Power, control and legitimacy are then located in the economic, technological, scientific, community and consumption systems (Beck, 1992). Beck argued that risk society copes through reflexivity, where both organisations and individuals engage in a process of reflexive self-monitoring, to scrutinise their production of risk and, in the case of individuals, to negotiate their way through an increasingly complex society where the influence of traditional institutions and social ties is diminishing. We *'collectively mediate our fears through what [Beck] called "reflexive modernisation"'* (Webb, 2006, p 2). Organisational openness and reflexivity is therefore crucial to generating trust and *stakeholder* involvement in the management of risk, regulating risk *'from within'* (Ramon, 2005, p 185). Those who cannot or do not conform are regulated to conform, to reduce risk and comply with expectations of the *'good citizen'* (ibid.). While Beck's thesis has been criticised for its suggestion that risk is indiscriminate (Scott, 2000) and for its emphasis on the decline of traditional, social structures (Rose, 1986), it remains relevant for a consideration of risk as an organising standard of social work, particularly given social work's duty to safeguard and address practices which present risks to self and others (HCPC, 2012). However, evidence suggests that social work has moved too far towards a rational, actuarial conceptualisation of risk, '*a statistical calculation… based upon aggregated data*' (Kemshall, 2010, p 1254)

Webb (2006) argues moreover that the limits of practice have become ever more narrow and reductive, governed by an outcome mentality, methods and techniques which ultimately de-skill practitioners and reduce their professional autonomy and discretion. While some argue that the profession's status and social workers' professionalism are protective factors (Evans, 2011), Webb suggests that social work is increasingly understood in instrumental, '*technical and functional terms*' (p 6). The influence of empiricism over aestheticism governs social work's current preference for '*technologies of care*' and *evidence* based on formal, normative assumptions and practice based on regulation (Gray and Webb, 2009, p 182). The value of knowledge and the skills of relationship have declined in preference for information and management (Parton, 2008). The only intelligence required is that which can '*be shared, quantified, accumulated and stored on a database*' (ibid., p 262). Knowledge of the subject, experience and meaning can get lost in reductionist systems of information capture and dissemination, with significant implications for personal identity. Virtual realities are created where the information on the screen can become more important than the actual person (Hayles, 1999). The impact of these virtual realities is particularly concerning if the person's uniqueness and humanity is already concealed behind vulnerability, risk and stigma, associated with personality disorder, for example. In effect, a data double can be constructed that takes on a life of its own (Haggerty and Ericson, 2000). Without knowledge, ideas and commitment and understanding, social work's ability to counter are restrained. The profession's responsibilities to address individual and collective challenges and enhance well-being (IFSW, 2014) and maintain trust and confidence (TCSW, 2012) are equally limited. Indeed, some have suggested the predominance of risk as a rational, calculable entity, open to regulation through information, and the electronic turn (Garret, 2005) has resulted in the McDonaldization of social work (Dustin, 2007). Preferring governance over intervention, the value attributed to face-to-face, expressive interaction has declined in favour of the procedurally routine (Webb, 2006). However, as Webb argues, social work is not without ethics, values and agency; it is not therefore incapable of rebalancing in favour of the subject, the relational, care and compassion (ibid.).

Social work, subject and relational

It would be wrong to deny social work's dependence on objective, rational knowledge and its role in the enforcement of social obligations (Parton, 2008). Indeed, as a member of the psy-complex, those professions orientated to medicine, psychiatry and psychology, social work has in part depended on scientific knowledge quite legitimately, in its role as a '*new instrument of government*' (Rose et al., 2009, p 8). Social work retains a role in what Foucault defined as governmentality: the distant governance of conduct by those authorised and responsible for what individuals '*do and for what happens to them*' (Foucault, 1997, p 68). Objective, scientific knowledge sustains professional intervention and expertise to direct human behaviour (ibid.). In this context it would be erroneous to refute the profession's need for the knowledge of this type. We are merely suggesting that social work is now over-reliant on the technical to solve problems and secure intended outcomes without a reciprocal reliance on the subject, social and relational. Fearful of the consequences for the people who use social work services, social workers and the profession more generally, knowledge of the subject and attention to the relationship we believe should be reclaimed.

Social work supports vulnerable people, often at fateful moments (Giddens, 2013) when their individual skills and strengths may be less visible. An over-reliance, at these times, on the rational and the technical can alienate and exclude the person, particularly if their capacities for self-monitoring are found wanting (Ramon, 2005). However, alienation from self and others only compounds personal powerlessness and inhibits professional control and autonomy. Some have argued, for example, that social work's over-reliance on the technical and managerial has induced a professional alienation, because control of the social work endeavour is subsumed to the demands of the database, with the analytical and discretionary skills of social workers marginalised (Ferguson and Lavalette, 2004; Parton, 2008). Indeed, some have argued that social work's persistent procedural reliance has and will continue to proletarianise social work, marginalising and de-skilling social workers in the process (Carey, 2007), without resistance, ie through attending to the importance of knowledge and relationship in understanding and realising the subject, ideas so evocative of social work's history and current value base.

Our professional value base (BASW, 2012; HCPC, 2012; TCSW, 2012) derives from a practical and theoretical heritage concerned with building meaningful relationships through which we might promote well-being and respond to threats (Ratcliffe, 1957). As social work's theoretical base was expanding out of a concern for the *social*, sociology, social policy and philosophy, Philip (1979) argued that knowledge should apprehend the individual, even those with vulnerabilities and presenting problems, as inherently social selves. In this regard social work would utilise skills of interpretation to give voice to the subject, underlying their '*objective status*', and thereby work to strengthen bonds of inclusive membership of society (Parton, 2008, p 255). Social work was more reliant on interpersonal and analytical skills to extract subjective knowledge and moreover engage the person in a process of change, of integration with family, community or wider society (ibid.). These ideas are relevant to any consideration of social work's current roles and responsibilities, particularly in relation to risk, given that the latter is a situated reality negotiated by service users and social workers alike as social actors (Kemshall, 2010). Risk is embedded in social situations and is imbued with both negative and positive connotations, '*consequently, risk may take a wide diversity of forms that reflect the purposes to which it is put and the assumptions on which it is based*' (O'Malley, 2008, p 453). As such, knowledge of the social and the subject, employed in a meaningful relationship, can aid social workers in their support of the person as they navigate the risks in their personal and social situation. Moreover, appreciating the situated nature of risk and the value of subject knowledge to understand it can lead to positive innovations, rather than '*what works*', but we can only get to the former through developing and sustaining relationships in unique, complex and challenging situations (Wilson et al., 2011).

Wilson et al. (2011) argue that it is relationships with service users that matter most. Through an effective, professional relationship social workers can appreciate the uniqueness and complexity of service users' lives and engage with them so that they can confront challenges and find a greater sense of well-being (IFSW, 2014). Relationship-based practice does not attempt to obscure the muddle and chaos of social life through overly technical means, but accepts the interdependency of both object and subject and how one is defined in relation to the other (Weber, 2012). Interpretation of context, language and meaning is important in the interplay between person and practitioner, as is the professional use of self and the social worker's ability to hold different perspectives or extremes in balance or creative tension (Wilson et al., 2011). Not only does this respect the person and their enablement (BASW, 2012), we gain knowledge of their perspective on their needs and risks, which in turn informs innovative practice to promote learning, perhaps through more positive risk taking (Ramon, 2005). Despite a seemingly inherent contradiction, relationship-based practice resonates with the needs and risks associated with personality disorder. Given it is associated with impairment in self and interpersonal functioning, with significant and enduring difficulties in at least two of the following areas – cognition, affect, interpersonal relationships and impulse control (APA, 2013) – extremes of thought, feelings and behaviours are more than likely. However, too heavy a reliance on form and the objective classification of symptoms can marginalise and stigmatise the subject, leading all concerned to believe that the person is responsible for their distress, thoughts, feelings and behaviours (Breeze and Repper, 1998). Practitioners who can balance form and content, the rational and the subjective in relation to each other, will appreciate that such expressive action can simply be a means by which the person is trying to cope with the intensity of their distress (Stalker et al., 2005). Knowledge of the subject gleaned through an effective, professional relationship can inform practice in this area, particularly in relation to risk and in this way challenge the stigma and discrimination which surrounds the diagnosis and thereby promote more humane responses to the person.

Utilising the goods of modernity, reflection and reflexivity can help us sustain a professional relationship in challenging circumstances, as reflecting both *in* and *on* action (Schon, 1983) empowers us to keep form and content, object and subject in balance. In conjunction with a genuinely reflexive approach which appreciates how individuals understand the world and their position in it (Finlay, 2002), we can perhaps more easily accept the messiness of social life, without recourse to those more technically rational defences and the risks that they bring (Wilson et al., 2011). However, reflective practitioners engaged in reflexive, relationship-based practice in any domain, but particularly in the world of personality disorder, require compatible organisational and management structures capable of withstanding and holding the tension between object, subject and tolerating the anxiety associated with sometimes risky, muddled and chaotic social lives (Ruch, 2012).

Management at the macro and micro

Earlier in this chapter we referred to New Labour's enthusiasm for modernising our relationship, as citizens, with the state and public services (Giddens, 1999). Key in the *modernising* of social work, Modernizing Social Services aimed to promote independence through high-quality services focused on protection, regulation and accountability to both standards and performance (DoH, 1998). With co-operation and partnership inherent within the Third Way, foundations for increased collaboration between statutory and non-statutory bodies were established (ibid.). The market for health and welfare services moved from its previous position of *quasi* to a more generally inclusive market of statutory and non-statutory, voluntary and private providers (Heffernan, 2006; DoH, 1990). Health and welfare services became increasingly orientated to consumer choice and public service management (Hood, 1991). Social work became increasingly orientated to the demands of New Public Management (NPM), with its emphasis on performance management, regulation through audit and inspection, and some have argued a robust management style full of machismo (Clarke and Newman, 1993). NPM appears to serve therefore as a new form of regulation in a risk society, another means of bolstering our fragile confidence in traditional mechanisms for control and accountability (Beck, 1992). Furthermore, it appears to fit with a policy context which prioritises public safety, control and service rationing, particularly given the former's attention to budget management (Berg et al., 2008). Indeed, NPM would appear to contextualise the predominance of the rational and technical in social work, at the risk of alienating the subject (Frisby, 1992). Advocates of NPM, however, suggest that it delivers on efficiency and accountability and therefore it can deliver improved public services, with greater empowerment of service users (Dent and Barry, 2004). Nonetheless, many have questioned NPM's fit with the primary task of social work, to '*respond to and help alleviate the distress experienced by individuals arising from their personal and social circumstances*' (Ruch, 2012, p 1322). While our primary task may be dynamic, contingent on norms, ideas and actions, Ruch argues that the one non-negotiable factor in the social work task is the '*central place of human beings*' (ibid., p 1322).

Interpreting and attending to the individual as a social being, giving voice to their uniqueness and the complexity of their situation, is perhaps not best served by a system which prioritises measurement and efficiency over knowledge and understanding. As one social worker has said, the '*constant sort of drive to indicate performances. I think the actual work is suffering because of that*' (Audit Commission, 2002, p 23) (cited in Berg et al., 2008, p 115). Increasingly separated from the unpredictability of practice, managers face accusations of insensitivity to the values of public service and the meeting of need (ibid.). Indeed, some have suggested that this separation from, or even denial of, the unpredictability of the social work task results in ever-increasing anxiety, fight or flight mentalities and defensive practice (Ruch, 2012). Interestingly, these consequences resonate with some less than helpful responses to personality disorder. We can tend to avoid or project thoughts, feelings and behaviours which challenge our personal and professional esteem. Unhelpful responses can, as we have suggested, foster alienation, escalate distress and possibly the risk to self or others (Watts and Morgan, 1994). Reflecting NIMHE's (2003) call for shared understandings about the nature of personality-related distress, Ruch (2012) also calls for shared understandings between managers and practitioners about the complexity of the social work task. With an emphasis on refection, reflexivity and the power of management founded on relational rather than the managerial principles, Ruch's argument values the social and subjective in both practice and management, as an important counterbalance to the rational and the objective. In application to social work practice with people with personality disorder, we would like to suggest that shared understandings, between managers, practitioners and people with personality disorder, would enhance well-being, reduce risk and challenge the alienation experienced in this area of practice. However, alliances and shared understandings have not traditionally been seen as conducive to work with people with personality disorder, given the need to maintain appropriate and professional boundaries for safe and effective practice (Norton, 2012, Chapter 15).

Social work standards, codes and ethics similarly emphasise the maintenance of professional boundaries (BASW, 2012), knowing the limits of practice and confidentiality in the establishment of personal and professional boundaries with individuals and professional colleagues (HCPC, 2012), all of which contribute to upholding and maintaining public trust and confidence in ways that merit trust (TCSW, 2012). We are not questioning this in any way, merely questioning as others have done, whether the adherence to professional boundaries has encouraged separation, rather than mutuality and shared understandings (O'Leary et al., 2013). Evidence suggests that boundary setting, within reductionist, technically rational structures, can encourage distance, separating professionals, including social workers, from their clients (ibid.). However, we know that distant responses can fail to reflect the awareness of the person's vulnerability and how they might require the *'protection of the bond'* (Downie, 2011, p 25). Weak bonds do not prioritise the care of the person, nor do they facilitate good communication, empathy or respect (Stern, 2004), features of more trusting partnerships between person and professional (Borman, 2011, pp 209–21). O'Leary et al. (2013) argue that it is the quality of our purposive and dynamic relationships with people using social work services that helps us to better cope with the diversity and complexity of their situations, needs and risks. Boundary setting becomes just one aspect of a purposive and dynamic relationship and should be grounded in a mutual understanding of the reasons for intervention, the transparent sharing of information, a commitment to complete tasks and sound interpersonal skills (ibid.). Openness and clarity about roles, expectations and boundaries have been found to be effective in fields where the *client* is involuntary or *difficult* to engage (Cherry, 2005; Trotter, 2004). Rather than threaten social work's duty to maintain trust and confidence through respecting professional limits, boundary setting grounded in mutuality, purpose and transparency appears to more than uphold social work's professional value base to ensure proficiency in the promotion of social justice and addressing discrimination, disadvantage and oppression (HCPC, 2012). It would seem that management and practice grounded in what is at stake in the lives of individuals and communities (Kleinman, 1999), that which generates shared understandings about the complexity and uniqueness of social life, offers more than those procedures which appear to reduce management and practice to the securing of efficient, affordable outcomes, performance and regulation. We would suggest therefore that the social and the relational holds significant sway in work with people with personality disorder, especially given the extent of stigma and discrimination they continue to endure (Tetley et al., 2012).

Conclusion

This chapter has analysed the implications of some of social work's key drivers, the rational and technical contrasted with the social and the relational. While always a feature in social work's history we have suggested that, in recent years, the former has dominated the latter. To call for a reversal of this trend, for the preeminence of the social and relational, would go against the ethos and spirit of this book. We are simply calling for greater symmetry between the two domains, so that social work might better work to its values and aims. Greater recognition of our interdependent social selves, as both rational and social actors negotiating the complexity of life in late modern society, would limit the objectification of less than desirable characteristics. Appreciating the humanity behind representative attributes, and/or vulnerabilities such as mental illness, would not only sustain our creative and reflective capacities, it would help challenge the alienation and exclusion of those who can come to be defined by their negative attributes. We are suggesting this holds particular relevance for those with a diagnosis of personality disorder, whom we know are often stereotyped as difficult and dangerous Others.

We have acknowledged, however, that policy has tended to support these normative assumptions that mental illness equates with dangerousness. We have suggested that policy has traditionally prioritised public safety and control, within a rational, neo-liberal drive for efficiency, over and above any emphasis on the acquisition of knowledge and understanding about the reasons for risk and the social situations which lie behind it. We are not denying risk, especially at fateful moments; indeed, we have some sympathy for Beck's original thesis. We are simply suggesting that appreciating risk as socially situated, rather than solely abstract, values knowledge of the subjective as a counterbalance to the rational and technical. Risks might be more easily balanced with strengths, safety with positive risk taking. While such dualities are part of social work's rich history, it is unfortunate, from our perspective, that social work has favoured a more rational actuarial conceptualisation of, and response to, risk in recent years. The focus of practice has narrowed; the influence of knowledge and interpersonal skills has declined in favour of information and management through systematic procedures. However, social work is not without agency, ethics and values and we agree the profession is more than capable of squaring its rational and social selves through greater articulation of its interpretative and analytical skills, understanding and realising the social, both individual and collective, thereby promoting greater social justice for those otherwise excluded for their seemingly negative attributes.

For us, relationship-based practice is key not only to social work squaring its own circle, but to social work practice with people with personality disorder. Founding practice on those products of modernity, reflection and reflexivity aids balance by helping us confront that which we would rather avoid. We know that personality disorder can induce extremes of thought, feelings and behaviour. We know that it can challenge both the professional and personal esteem of mental health professionals, including MHSWs. We would suggest, however, that attending to knowledge, gained from the subject, through the use of our interpersonal skills would foster interpretation and those necessary mutual understandings about the context and reasons for the person's distress. We might then realise more empathic understandings for those who are quite frequently defined as failed. Relationship-based practice in this context demands certain prerequisites, professional boundaries more suited to dynamic, purposive practice, support and management more suited to the primary task, the centrality of the person and what is at stake for them. However, we would suggest the benefits of this effort outweigh the costs, as it would realise MHSWs' part in securing better outcomes for people with personality disorder through an appreciation of form, content, object and subject in equal measure.

Summary points

- Reciprocity is important.

- Balance between form, content, the technical and the subjective is significant.

- Reflection and reflexivity are useful tools, helping us negotiate the dichotomies of life.

- Management and practice should reflect the primary task of social work: what is at stake for individuals, groups and communities.

- Relationship-based practice has much to offer MHSWs supporting people with personality disorder.

Taking it further

Gray, M and Webb, S (2013) *The New Politics of Social Work*. London: Palgrave.

Hardy, M (2015) *Governing Risk: Care and Control in Contemporary Social Work*. London: Palgrave.

Parker, J and Stanworth, H (2015) *Explaining Social Life: A Guide to Using Social Theory*. London: Palgrave.

Parton, N and O'Byrne, P (2000) *Constructive Social Work: Towards a New Practice*. London: Palgrave.

Ruch, G (2010) *Relationship Based Social Work*. London: Jessica Kingsley.

4 Research findings: working to empower a response to trauma

Critical questions

» *How does a social perspective on personality disorder connect with current health and well-being agendas?*

» *What is a social perspective on personality disorder?*

» *How can understanding trauma inform humane, empathic relationships?*

» *How can knowledge of the person inspire the professional use of self?*

» *How can the relational inspire broad social supports to promote connection and reconnection?*

Introduction

Our suggestion of a current weighting in practice, towards the technical and rational, should not imply ignorance of the indicators of more positive change. Indeed, the shift towards supporting and promoting well-being through integrated ways of working, based on strengths rather than deficits, involving supported self-assessment and a right to independent advocacy (DoH, 2014), nicely contextualises a different approach to working with people with personality disorder. Policy specific to mental health services similarly reflects attention to the voice and rights of people with mental health issues, learning disability and autism (DoH, 2015a). With a drive to improve the life chances of vulnerable people, so that they may exercise more choice and control in their lives, the emphasis once again is on working to strengths to deliver better outcomes (ibid.). Remarkably, social work is allotted a specific responsibility within this most recent of policies. Each person receiving a service as a result of a mental health, learning disability or developmental need, will have a named social worker to deliver professional advice and support, as the primary contact for the person and their family, offering a professional voice across services (ibid.). This development is somewhat unexpected given evidence of the apparent contraction of social work within mental health services (SCIE, 2008), with the former frequently needing to explain and defend its role (Campbell et al., 2006; O'Brien and Calderwoood, 2010). Nonetheless, with an anticipated rollout in 2016–17 the policy offers MHSW an opportunity to galvanise its contribution to mental health services and reassert the importance of a social perspective in understanding the contributors and consequences of mental disorder. We would suggest that nowhere is this more needed than in the area of personality disorder.

The knowledge and skills of social workers grounded as they are in '*human dignity, service to humanity and social justice*' (Bisman, 2004, p 109) orientate both candidate and qualified social workers to people's strengths and the exercise of choice and control as active citizens (DoH, 2015b). Proficiency in the professional use of self, interpersonal skills and emotional intelligence enables social workers to establish effective, transparent relationships with vulnerable people so as to support them both practically and emotionally (ibid.). However, social workers are required to negotiate these relationships with professionalism, so as to ensure the maintenance of personal and professional boundaries (BASW, 2015b). Experienced social workers are expected to promote and advance an individual's autonomy and self-determination while advocating for their human and civil rights (ibid.). Required to recognise the impact of socio-economic, psychological, environmental and physiological factors, social workers accept the importance of relationships for people and should understand the centrality of loss, change, separation, attachment and resilience in people's lives. The knowledge, skills and aptitudes of social workers enable skilful and confident communication and engagement with people in complex, and sometimes unpredictable, situations (BASW, 2015). Given the extremes of distress experienced by people with personality disorder (Castillo, 2003), social work knowledge, skills and capabilities appear therefore an appropriate and useful source of support for people with the diagnosis. However, evidence suggests that while social workers work with people with personality disorder, there is an absence of specific social work research, which suggests that social work is potentially operating in '*an educational vacuum*' in this area (Keys and Lambert, 2002, p 4). The dearth of social work research, as substantiated by our own literature searches over the course of a decade, was a catalyst for the research project which has subsequently inspired this book. The next section will explain this project's rationale, set it in context and summarise its methodology.

The research project

The project explored MHSW practice from the perspective of both service users with personality disorder and MHSWs. It sought to answer three research questions: how service users with personality disorder and MHSWs understand the diagnosis; how they understand MHSW practice in the area; and finally how they think MHSW practice might be better informed.

These questions emerged from my experience as a qualified MHSW in social work teams, community mental health services and most recently a forensic, medium-secure service for people with personality disorder. It was while working within community mental health services in the late 1990s that I first became aware of how we, as mental health professionals, can stigmatise people with personality disorder and effectively deny them access to support and treatment. This was hard for me to witness and absorb, whether unintentional or not. However, my observations made me question how we, as professional MHSWs, understand personality disorder and whether our knowledge of the disorder is sufficient. If we understood the nature of the distress, surely we would respond more positively to the person? These questions were strengthened by the narratives I heard, while working in a forensic service, from patients describing how they had previously been excluded from mental health services and how, from their perspective, any access to treatment had invariably led to misdiagnosis and treatment inappropriate to their needs. I became increasingly aware of how offending behaviour could, for some, be a means of help-seeking behaviour. Given that early childhood adversity and preadmission offending can be related for some patients (Jones et al., 2010), many of the patients' explanations for their offending and subsequent detention held some veracity for me.

While patients' experiences of stigma and discrimination within mental health services fitted with my previous observations, they appeared unjust and led me to conclude that people with personality disorder face a disproportionate risk of stigma, discrimination and exclusion. This personal conclusion was supported soon after by the publication of the NIMHE (2003) guidance challenging the exclusion surrounding personality disorder. Such support for my personal observations motivated me to explore the literature further, hoping that I would find more support for my own conclusions. As a member of a profession committed to non-discriminatory practice, promoting social justice and addressing the impact of discrimination, disadvantage and oppression (BASW, 2015a), I anticipated social work literature in the area. However, while I found an extensive range of psychiatric and psychological literature, I was extremely disappointed by the relative absence of specific social work literature catering especially to personality disorder. However, this discovery gave me the impetus to initiate, enrol and register a project, which over the course of the following ten years, from start to finish, would investigate personality disorder from an MHSW perspective.

The project emerged from my experiences as a professional MHSW, first, from my observations about how people with personality disorder can be excluded from mental health services, despite experiencing distress which can be extreme and overwhelming; second, from the apparent lack of specific social work research in this area, despite the prevalence of personality disorder in both primary and secondary settings (Newton-Howes et al., 2010); and, finally, from my interest in how understanding influences behaviour. I was and still am motivated by different ways of knowing (Fawcett and Featherstone, 1999, pp 5–24) to generate different understandings and ultimately different, more positive responses to the person with personality disorder. I had been committed to service user involvement and the development of practice through collaboration between service users and practitioners throughout my career (Beresford and Croft, 2001; Ramon et al., 2004). It was therefore essential for me to include an expert by experience perspective (Fox, 2008). Involving both service user and MHSW participants in a project, in an under-researched area for social work, seemed an ideal opportunity to better inform practice through collaboration, albeit in a virtual sense. Consequently, these interests and commitments influenced the design of the project, particularly the decision to ask service users for their ideas about how practice might be better informed and to put these ideas to MHSW participants in the second phase of the research. The next section will summarise the project's theoretical foundations and methodology.

Theoretical foundations

You will have seen in the previous section that the project's research questions were oriented to the *how*; how service users and MHSWs understand and experience personality disorder and MHSW practice. I as the researcher would be immersed in participants' interpretations and experiences, negotiating my way through similarities, differences and contradictions. Consequently, the research design and methodology had to help explain the relative nature of human experience and appreciate this very experience as a source of knowledge, while enabling proximity to the source without compromising or contradicting bias and research ethics (D'Cruz and Jones, 2004). The project should be seen perhaps as an example of interpretivist research, offering insights into the nature of personality disorder and MHSW practice. Postmodern, constructivist and critical ideas were important theoretical underpinnings because they enabled me to deal with the complex and contested disposition of personality disorder (Winship and Hardy, 2007), with its many different ways of knowing and understanding. I hoped that by investigating the different perspectives, of service users and MHSWs, the project might help challenge the seemingly dominant but negative construction of personality disorder (NIMHE, 2003) and ultimately help to generate better outcomes for those with the diagnosis. Research methodology therefore had to pay attention to the process of the research and the meanings of participants and mine as researcher (Denzin and Lincoln, 2008).

Methodology

A qualitative methodology with purposeful sampling and active, semi-structured interviews fitted with the project's research questions and underpinning foundations and in turn would support my understanding and interpretation of participants' meanings. Semi-structured interviews would allow flexibility, but with a more active stance both researcher and participant can engage in *'meaning making'* (Holstein and Gubrium, 2004, p 149). Both actors have a part to play, with the researcher positioned as the *traveller* asking *'questions that lead the subjects to tell their own stories of their lived world'* (Kvale, 1996, p 4). As such a more active interview fitted with the project's aims, theoretical foundations and methodology. However, while such collaborative research interviews (Holstein and Gubrium, 2004) balance the *how* of the interview process with the *what* of lived experience, they run the risk of encouraging bias and researcher over-involvement (Rubin and Rubin, 1995). I would, therefore, need a strategy to account for my influence on the fieldwork which ultimately involved 10 interviews with service users and 12 with MHSWs between 2007 and 2012.

I organised the data collection in two phases: Phase 1 interviews with service users, Phase 2 interviews with MHSWs. Interviews with service users took place between May 2007 and February 2008. Sampling for this phase was purposeful and qualitative as the sample could be described as *'hard to reach'* (Lee, 1993). It was this reason which motivated me to employ an outcropping strategy, whereby I found a *'site in which its members congregate to study them there'* (Lee, 1999, p 69). While outcropping risks dependency on one research site and therefore a restricted, homogeneous sample (Lee, 1999), it enables the researcher to get close to hard-to-reach and perhaps even vulnerable participants (Involve, 2004). Ethical review was imperative and extensive.

Phase 1 was reviewed by a University Faculty Research Ethics Committee (FREC). I was guided in this by the Research Governance Framework (DoH, 2005c) which outlines principles of good governance and other key organisations of relevance (Social Research Association [SRA], 2003). I am confident that the research was conducted in ways that protected participants from harm, breach of confidentiality and identification. Protection from harm was particularly pertinent in this phase, given participants' potential vulnerability. An inclusion and exclusion criterion was an integral part of protecting potential participants from harm. It stipulated that service users who had been detained under the Mental Health Act (MHA) (DoH, 1983), those who had been voluntary patients in the previous six months and those who had had a crisis-related respite in the previous six weeks, would be excluded from participating in the research. Furthermore, at FREC's request I devised, with the facilitator, an agreement about what would happen should a service user become distressed during the interview.

Phase 2 entailed 12 interviews with MHSWs from three different areas of the UK between 2010 and 2012. I had hoped to employ an outcropping strategy in this phase also, via a national social work organisation. However, when this was thwarted for a number of reasons, I reverted to a more straightforwardly purposeful strategy, exploiting established local and national networks in order to get the buy-in of key gatekeepers. Ultimately I interviewed eight MHSWs from a trust in the East of England, two from a local authority in the North West and two from a Trust in the North East of England. Again, ethical review was extensive, partly as a result of the different geographies within the sample. Phase 2 was reviewed and approved by both the FREC and NHS Ethics and Research and Development bodies. Phase 2 again involved an element of criterion sampling: a simple inclusion and exclusion criteria, which included social workers with experience of working with personality disorder and excluded those who did not.

Interviewing was supplemented by a purposeful, documentary analysis of policies key to furthering my understanding of both personality disorder (DoH, 1983, 1999b, 2007; DoH and Home Office, 1992) and social work (DoH, 1998, 1999a, 2006). My use of documentary sources fitted the project's relativist, subjectivist and inductive nature. However, it was also an important feature of bias management in the method and *doing* of the research, triangulating data and exploring understandings and experiences of personality disorder and MHSW practice. Consequently, documentary analysis offered a counterpoint to the data gathered from service users and MHSWs and so supported my reflexive approach to the management of bias throughout the research process (Atkinson and Coffey, 1997).

Reflexivity seeks to appreciate how individuals understand the world and their position in it (Finlay, 2002). It also helps the researcher to negotiate his or her proximity to participants' meanings and the complexities in the research relationship, including bias. There were a number of reasons why such an approach was important. First, I have my own interpretive frame. My experiences of working with people with personality disorder as an MHSW influenced the development of the research questions, the design of the project, my commitment to it and the lens through which I would view it and research participants. Second, I was aware of my status as a former MHSW and how this might influence participants' view of me, their decisions about whether to participate and their responses to my questions if they did. Finally, the project's subjectivist epistemology and inductive methodology would draw me close to participants' meanings. I needed strategies to help me negotiate this proximity, to help ensure that I did not over-interpret the data or a particular part of it. Consequently, I made good use of my research diary together with member checking of transcripts, team and peer researcher critique of samples of my data analysis, all of which helped me to reflect on the content of interview data and interrogate my interaction with it, and helped me to guard against bias in the design and method of the research.

Design and methodology had to help explain the relative nature and experience of personality disorder and MHSW, valuing this experience as a source of knowledge. Theoretical foundations were critical and postmodern, methodology qualitative and purposeful, to support my ethical, reflexive approach and achieve my objectives of gaining an authentic understanding of personality disorder in an MHSW context. You might question why this was necessary. Its necessity stemmed from an apparent paucity of personality disorder literature and research specific to or for MHSW. The next section will summarise the existing literature I have found so as to contextualise the findings from this project, which suggest the importance of understanding personality disorder as a response to trauma, key relational skills and social interventions to support people with the diagnosis.

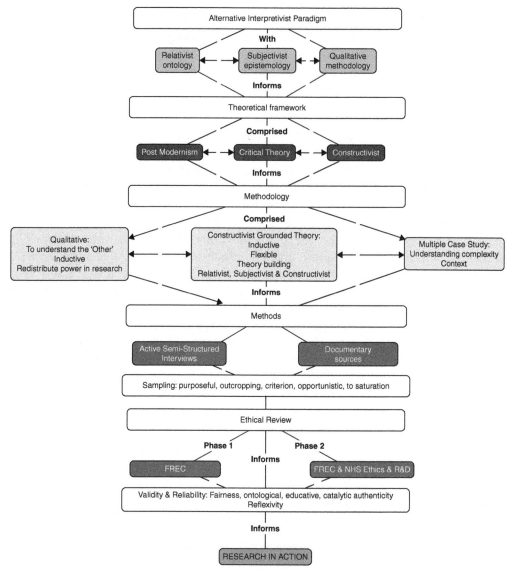

Figure 4.1 Paradigm, theory, methodology and methods

Existing MHSW literature

A small body of specific empirical literature both delineates important themes about how personality disorder is experienced and, crucially, establishes the importance of consistency, practical support and networking (Burton, 1990; Irvine, 1996) in support of the person with the diagnosis. However, the challenges for MHSWs are clear: from being unprepared for the nature of the work (Burton, 1990) to overcoming professional anxiety about the efficacy of the MHSW skill set (Titus, 2004). This small body of work highlights how people with personality disorder experience difficulties in family and social relationships and consequently are often lonely, socially isolated and stigmatised (Burton, 1990; Irvine, 1996; Titus, 2004). Interestingly, all point to the experience of disadvantage or trauma as a precursor to personality disorder. However, the potential of MHSW to support people with personality disorder is clear. Burton (1990) suggests the relevance of goal-orientated work, particularly that associated with practical tasks and liaison or networking with others. Irvine (1996) similarly picks up on the importance of MHSWs supporting people to maintain their tenancy. Consistency in relationships to build trust can help the person to reflect on the nature of their relationships with self and others and offer opportunities to reinforce positive behaviours (Burton, 1990).

However, in later research involving MHSW participants, Stalker et al. (2005) identify how inconsistency in service provision can undermine trust and therefore perhaps the efficacy of professional relationships. It appears that the efficacy of social work skills and interventions in this area would be better supported by greater preparation on the part of MHSWs, so that they are perhaps more resilient to withstand the challenges within the work (Burton, 1990). Conversely, with scant attention to personality disorder in the MHSW literature base (Keys and Lambert, 2002), adequate preparation and knowledge might be a challenge (Titus, 2004). Furthermore, Irvine (1996) identifies how both people with personality disorder and multidisciplinary colleagues can hold unrealistic expectations of social work staff, which interestingly can leave social workers feeling isolated and alone with the work and the burden of constant crises. Titus (2004) argues that social work needs to adopt a more proactive response to people with personality disorder, rooted in a social model of disability, emphasising the individual's competence and knowledge of their own strengths and deficits and a belief in social work's skills and competence (BASW, 2015b; HCPC, 2012). We saw in Chapter 2 how the social model is a contested concept in its own right (Beresford, 2002). However, we have suggested its value for understanding possible causes and consequences of personality disorder. Herein lays the catalyst for the research project at the heart of this book: the belief in the value of a social perspective for understanding the lived experience of personality disorder despite the scarcity of MHSW research and literature in the area. It was important therefore that the analysis of research data culminated in a product, a grounded theory to help explain the experience of personality disorder and MHSW practice.

A grounded theory study

Grounded Theory (GT) (Glaser and Strauss, 1967) is both a method and the product of inquiry. As a method it is flexible, enabling the researcher '*to focus their data collection and to build inductive middle-range theories through successive levels of data analysis and conceptual development'* (Charmaz, 2008, p 204). Constant Comparative Method (CCM) and simultaneous data collection/analysis (Glaser and Strauss, 1967) aid the analysis of processes and the researcher's proximity to the studied world (Glaser, 2002). Grounded theory enabled the generation of a theory relevant to personality disorder and MHSW practice. Simultaneous data collection and analysis would enable me to get as close as possible to participants' unique meanings and thereby ensure the research product – the grounded theory – was relevant to the data, personality disorder and MHSW practice (Glaser and Strauss, 1967). However, in its original form GT would challenge the project's relativist and subjectivist foundations. The work of Charmaz (2008) became increasingly important to the process and product of the research.

Constructivist Grounded Theory shares GT's interest in processes, adheres similarly to CCM and concurrent data collection and analysis and shares GT's inductive theory-building capabilities. However, CGT prioritises the studied world rather than the methods for studying it and is consequently founded on more relativist assumptions about *reality* and the value of experience as a source of knowledge. CGT fitted therefore with the project's theoretical and methodological foundations and would help me to account for my own '*interpretive frame of reference*' (ibid., p 206). It also fitted with my more active interviewing stance as it allows the researcher to be much more present in the process of collecting or generating data and in the reporting of the research (Mills et al., 2006), underlining the importance of a reflexive approach (Finlay, 2002).

In answering the first two research questions, the project generated a grounded theory, represented in Figure 4.1, suggesting that personality disorder is related to early traumatic experience which impacts on the person throughout the life course (Erikson, 1968). Intense emotional distress can alienate the person from themselves and others and lead to extreme and unsafe behaviours. The theory suggests that humane, empathic and prosocial relationships can interrupt the cycle of malignant alienation and help manage the risk of a fatal outcome (Watts and Morgan, 1994). The theory values courage in the face of adversity, our commonality as human beings and the particular relevance of MHSW's ability to work with the person in their environment and their abilities to use self to communicate, engage and take an active interest in the person. Furthermore, broad social interventions such as practical support, encouragement and liaison with others can help MHSW to empower the person's more constructive response to traumatic experience. As such this theory suggests that MHSW has a role to play in a more balanced and holistic response to people with personality disorder through which it will articulate its unique contribution to multidisciplinary mental health services.

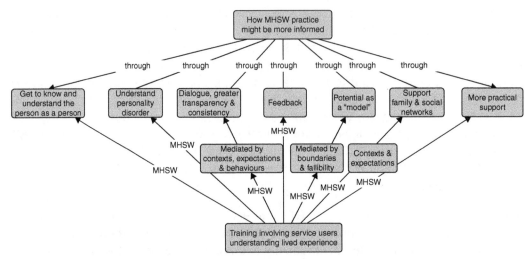

Figure 4.2 How MHSW might promote connections and more positive responses to trauma.

Understandings of personality disorder

Research data from both phases indicates how personality disorder resists singular explanation and is in fact a complex, multifaceted phenomena, which if misunderstood can have significant implications for service users and those who work with them. Service users in Phase 1 reported how, in their experience, personality disorder is heterogeneous rather than discrete and can therefore often be confused with other illnesses and diagnoses. One participant described her different diagnoses before acquiring one of personality disorder, '*I've been named with quite a few illnesses – schizophrenia, bi-polar, all different things, but in the end they come up with personality disorder*' (27 June 2007). Reflecting similarities in this data, some MHSWs suggested that personality disorder doesn't sit well within the medical model, nor does it fit with the latter's treatment assumptions as '*they can't give you anything*' for personality disorder (Phase 1, 27 June 2007). One MHSW (16 March 2010) commented on how personality disorder is '*not something that is necessarily caused by a chemical imbalance, something biological, physiological, whatever you want to call it*' but more related to lived experience, more about how certain '*individuals have to negotiate their way through life*' (Phase 2, 24 November 2010).

Interestingly, MHSW data reflects the uncertainty surrounding the diagnosis, about whether it sits on a continuum with other mental state disorders (WHO, 1992) or is a discrete category in itself (APA, 1994). Moreover, some suggested that the relativity of experience, together with the number of theoretical interpretations which surround it, can both '*shed light*' and *obscure*. One MHSW described how '*we've all got personalities; we could all be seen as having a disorder because what I might think is perfectly ok, something might think, "Oh, that's a bit odd of her"*' (Phase 2, 18 May 2010). Four MHSWs suggested that complexity can impair professional confidence and understanding. Service users question, quite correctly it seems, if MHSWs and mental health professionals, more generally, don't understand the diagnosis, how can they offer the much-needed explanations? Nine out of the ten service users interviewed had not received a meaningful explanation of personality disorder, and five of these had received no explanation at all. One service user (Phase 1, 27 June 2007) was given a diagnosis of BPD in hospital, but no one explained it to her: *'No, they didn't tell me anything. I only learnt from here really'*. Reflecting the importance of informed explanations, one MHSW argues that *'unless you explain to them what that means and what can be done about it, it's better you just didn't tell them'* (Phase 2, 16 March 2010).

A lack of explanation appears only one consequence of confused understanding, as the latter also appears to fuel negative and distant responses to the person. Data from Phase 1 indicates how service users with personality disorder can be ignored and set apart by professionals and mental health services. The stigma associated with personality disorder can contribute to negative stereotypes and can legitimise a professional distance, which in turn can reinforce distress, exclusion and the sense of the person's apartness from the mainstream. Data from both samples resonates with similarities on this, with service users describing *professional* responses governed by rejection, resignation, fear and denial which, in turn, contribute to the particular stigma surrounding the diagnosis, associated as it is with violence and constructed as a *'dustbin diagnosis'* (Beresford, 2005). Comparably, data from Phase 2 indicates how personality disorder is not seen *'as the business of mental health services'* and as a consequence the service response to the person can be framed by either resignation, fear or denial (01 June 2010). Essentially, data from both phases indicates how MHSWs and service users with personality disorder can construct each other as the 'Other' (Spalek, 2007).

'Othering' in action

Othering is best conceptualised as a process by which we differentiate in order to both defend against risk or threat and maintain a positive identity, whether collectively or individually (Rohleder, 2007). Resonant of psychoanalytical theory, Othering illuminates how we learn to split good from bad at a very young age in order to preserve the good, both in ourselves and others and defend against the bad (Klein, 1959). However, although protective on the one hand, the process is not without consequence, particularly for those defined as the Other. We would suggest appreciating Othering as a process requires an understanding of the ways in which ideas about self are governed by the contexts in which they are embedded (Rose, 1986; Sampson, 2003). Western economies require rational, self-contained individuals (Geertz, 1977), and those who are different or perceived as such, dependent and seemingly less rational, can so easily be seen and defined as the Other (Young, 1999). We appear to employ such defences at times of stress and/or threat (Segal, 1992). We must defend at these times, if not, the self is threatened psychologically and physically (Wright et al., 2007). A principal defence is to deny *our* commonality as human beings by denying *them* their humanity (Young, 1999). However, those so denied can through a process of projective identification come to internalise and adopt negative projections to see themselves through the lens of their beholders (Klein, 1959).

Although more recent policy perhaps underplays any consideration of personality disorder, particularly in relation to access to services (DoH, 2009, 2010), earlier policy describes how those with the diagnosis can be constructed as the demonised Other (Wright et al., 2007), excluded from mental health services (NIMHE, 2003). Data from Phase 2 supports such constructions, in that MHSWs report that the person can be perceived as difficult, failed, problematic and unworthy, *'they're just seen as a problem sometimes, yeah as the problem, somebody that is really just, "it's their own fault"; it's very judgemental type thing: "Why don't they just pull themselves together?"'* (Phase 2, 13 April 2010). The literature suggests that while appointing the person responsible for their own distress is a consequence of stigma (Goffman, 1990), attribution of responsibility and blame can serve as a professional defence protecting the professional or MHSW from the intensity of the person's distress (Bateman and Fonagy, 2004), which challenges both personal and professional esteem (Hinshelwood, 1999). Defence and therefore distance is viewed as legitimate. However, the distance, which serves to protect, can compound negative conceptions of self, escalate the distance between person and professional and ultimately compromise the efficacy of professional support and intervention. A process of malignant alienation is set in play, *'a progressive deterioration in their relationships with others, including loss of sympathy and support from members of staff'* (Morgan, 1979, cited in Watts and Morgan, 1994, p 11). Relationships without hope, humanity or empathy distance the individual and encourage the internalisation of negative labels and emotions, ultimately escalating the risk of a fatal outcome for the person (Watts and Morgan, 1994). Data from this project highlights how the distanced service user can in turn deny the humanity of the MHSW.

Data from Phase 1 reports how MHSWs risk being *sacked* by the person with personality disorder if they fail to take an interest in the person or engage in meaningful dialogue. One service user (09 January 2008) asserts how her MHSW, *'was useless, she did abso-lutely … she just used to come in every so often, are you all right, blah-blah-blah, "you've got a psychiatrist appointment this day, alright? Goodbye!" That's all she did'*. While such mechanisms may defend the MHSW against intense distress and feelings of inadequacy on their part, they appear to contradict expectations that a professional service is deliv-ered through a relationship that involves both a constructive bond and a caring attitude (Downie, 2011, pp 23–35). Findings suggest that MHSWs' attitudes and responses can be distant and ineffective and can fail to reflect awareness of the person's vulnerability and how this might require the *'protection of the bond'* (ibid., p 25). Weak bonds do not prioritise the care of the person, nor do they facilitate good communication, empathy or respect (Stern, 2004), features of more trusting partnerships between person and profes-sional (Borman, 2011, pp 209–21). They can therefore lead to ineffective support and negative constructions of the MHSW and/or mental health professional. MHSWs can be reduced to *liars*, only there to *'fob you off'* (Phase 1, 27 June 2007). While these construc-tions reflect service users' projections about their own fallibility and unpredictability, data suggests that they stem from MHSWs' distant and dismissive responses to the person. One participant (Phase 1, 09 January 2008) described how her MHSW made her *'feel very small sometimes'* and consequently what she said had little impact, as she would *'just do it for the visit and then go back to my old ways when she'd gone'*. We would suggest that understanding personality disorder more as a response to trauma might help restore the humanity of those with the diagnosis and more positive constructions of professionals, including MHSWs, trying to support them.

Understanding personality disorder as a response to trauma

We suggested in Chapter 2 the importance of trauma to a re-conceptualisation of personality disorder. While accepting that trauma is not yet recognised as an antecedent of the disorder, we suggested sufficient evidence exists to indicate its relevance for better understanding the experience of living with personality disorder (Ball and Links, 2009; Castillo, 2003; Lanius et al., 2010). We argued for a rebalancing in the form and content of distress (Bracken and Thomas, 2004), with priority accorded to the significance of destructive social experience, which may in turn generate greater empathy for the person with personality disorder. As such, we might then appreciate the trauma survivor's courage for battling, often alone, in the face of overwhelming adversity. Courage is often context dependent. Reframing the person as a courageous survivor might trigger curiosity about the context in which their courage became necessary. As one MHSW described in Phase 2, 'most of the people I've worked with, who have that label of personality disorder, are adult survivors of childhood abuse of some kind or another' (13 April 2010).

Service users in Phase 1 explained personality disorder as related to traumatic experience including that experienced in early life. Five participants suggested that personality disorder relates to difficult and traumatic experiences. One (Phase 1, 20 June 2007) described learning to live with 'just being really traumatised, and I actually learned to live with that, that was it'. Four service users asserted a relationship to earlier trauma, as one describes here: 'I find it a very self-destructive part of my life. It is a part of my life where something has happened and it's like some shock therapy, something has happened way, way back that has now affected me in adulthood' (Phase 1, 09 January 2010). One service user made a connection between past experiences as 'an ex-military man' and Post-Traumatic Stress Disorder (PTSD).

Similarly, 11 out of the 12 MHSWs connected personality disorder with difficult or traumatic past experiences, defined as childhood sexual abuse (Phase 2, 13 April 2010), physical and emotional abuse (Phase 2, 12 May 2010). One MHSW suggested a relationship between certain forms of abuse and certain personality disorders. One (Phase 2, 25 May 2010) described how personality disorder, 'seems to stem from some trauma: most of the service users I've worked with who have been given a label of personality disorder have had quite difficult childhoods: there's been abuse on some levels, both emotional and sometimes physical and sexual'. Such experiences can lead to extreme behaviours, as one MHSW (Phase 2, 24 November 2010) suggested, 'often the roots of those are from early childhood experiences, traumatic childhood experiences. And it leads to them perhaps taking sort of extreme action such as threatening suicide or self-harming, responding in various sort of aggressive disproportionate ways to requests'. Interestingly, one MHSW connected personality disorder with PTSD: 'I didn't understand the impact, didn't understand either for a long, long time about the trauma aspect. I know it is part of PTSD' (Phase 2, 13 April 2010).

We suggest therefore some commonality across both samples on the importance of trauma for understanding personality disorder. There is in addition an intriguing similarity across both samples in understanding the experience of personality disorder. Service user participants described the experience of distress as centred on loss, isolation, overwhelming emotions, intense reactions, pattern behaviour and projections. Distress can be complex, frightening and overwhelming, and life chaotic and risky, as one service user (Phase 1, 24 July 2007) conveys: '*I was really crying and crying and crying and really upset about it and things. I don't know: just different things that … My head's like a CD at times: it whizzes round from one thing to another. I was crying and crying and crying.*' Some MHSWs report that personality disorder can mean loss of the family, loneliness and isolation. It is perhaps no surprise that MHSWs perceive the enormity of a person's distress as one described:

> *when somebody's saying they're going to kill themselves over and over again, you know, it's not a nuisance, it's that they really don't know how to deal with the emotions and how to express it in a way that helps them manage it and reduces the anxiety that goes with it.*
>
> (Phase 2, 25 May 2010)

There is perhaps a dyad here, with expression and behaviour as both demonstration of survival and a desperate cry for help. Tew (2002) argues extreme behaviours, although risky, '*constitute both an awesome story of survival in relation to an oppressive or "unliveable" situation, and a desperate cry for help and understanding*' (p 147). Such a perspective prioritises dialogue and reciprocity, with the professional – the MHSW – positioned as an '*enlightened witness*' (ibid., p 150). Data from this research project suggests the importance of relational bonds, based on the knowledge of the person and their experience and social interventions, such as practical support, encouragement and '*being alongside*' and effective liaison with others in the person's social and professional network. We would suggest that such prosocial approaches can empower the person's response to trauma and promote connection and reconnection, which as we know can be the antidote to trauma (Herman, 1992). The next section will summarise research findings which indicate the importance of relational skills in the support of people with personality disorder.

The importance of helpful attitudes and caring bonds

In previous chapters we have outlined the importance of maintaining a balance between the form and content of distress and between objective and subjective states. We suggested that when form and object outweigh the content of distress and its subjective experience, stigma accumulates. We know that this is particularly the case with personality disorder and we have evidence of the destructive consequences for the person and those who care for them (Castillo, 2003; NIMHE, 2003). While social work has a history of attending to the social and the relational, components which undercut stigma and stigmatised responses, we know that mental health professionals, including social workers, can stigmatise people with personality disorder more frequently and to a greater degree than the general public (Latalova et al., 2015). We have considered how perhaps in recent years social work practice has become increasingly orientated to the technical and rational (Dustin, 2007), utilising risk management technology and routinising decision making (Ellis, 2014).

However, practice more orientated to the technical appears only to compound alienation and distance within the professional relationship and thereby escalate risk to self and others (Watts and Morgan, 1994; Wright et al., 2007). Reciprocity in social work's technologies of practice, the technical *and* the relational, would appear to better support our ability to identify risk to self and others, while also helping people to live with risk and uncertainty in their everyday lives (Wilson, 2006). Social work's standards and values ground the profession in strengthening society's bonds, enabling the voice of the vulnerable while engaging individuals, groups and communities in action for change (DoH, 2015b; Parton, 2008). The findings from this research project support such a view, that practice which attends to interpretation, meaning and the interpersonal will nourish caring bonds to promote better outcomes for people with personality disorder.

Data from Phase 1 indicates the importance of MHSW knowledge, of both person and personality disorder, the professional use of self, respect, listening and active engagement with the person as features of more caring bonds between person and MHSW. Knowledge of the person was critical for some service users, as the more the MHSW knows someone, the more *'they help me'* (20 June 2007). However, knowledge of the person should not be exercised to control or take a hold of the person, as one service user comments here: *'They've perhaps always got a hold over you and will always have that for the rest of your life ... I'm not quite sure, you're not in control of the life you lead'* (Phase 1, 24 July 2007). Knowledge of the person should be balanced with a reciprocal knowledge of the diagnosis, which interestingly might on occasion be a protective factor for MHSWs, helping to sustain their involvement in the face of a person's intense and overwhelming distress, as one service user comments, *'[she] has known me for quite a while now and she does understand personality disorder. So she can deal with it. Whenever I say something outrageous or I've done something, she goes, "Oh, that doesn't shock me!" [Laughs]'* (Phase 1, 24 July 2007). Knowledge of both person and diagnosis was important for MHSWs too, as without both, honesty and transparency will be impaired and perhaps more importantly the MHSW will be unable to *'actually spend some time working through how it [personality disorder] affects them and why'* (Phase 2, 13 April 2010).

MHSW knowledge grounds the professional use of self to articulate respect, listening and engagement with the person. Data from Phase 1 indicates the importance of the MHSW's commitment to listening and evidencing respect for service users as people, by getting involved. For some the most important aspect was how the MHSW *'came across'*, *'I think they've got to come across ... For me, personally, the biggest thing is I've got to be able to communicate with them so they can't do anything'* (Phase 1, 24 July 2007). Evidencing a proactive interest was important too, by going the *'extra mile'* (Phase 1, 10 July 2007) or getting things done, *'if she was going to do something, she'd do it that day. And if she was with me ... she'd be on the phone with me. She got on the phone in my house, making that phone call, get it done there and then'* (ibid.). MHSWs in Phase 2 similarly emphasise the importance of a positive, professional relationship built on mutual respect as this quote highlights, *'the very first thing I try to provide is a positive relationship where they experience actual stability and to a large degree, approval, and that constancy is there before anything else'* (Phase 2, 01 June 2010). Knowledge, use of self and interprofessional skills offer a foundation for the MHSW as a solid and reliable presence, the importance of which we will consider in the next chapter.

Attending to the relational in practice in this area may appear contradictory given what we know of how challenging relationships with self and others are for people with the disorder

(APA, 2013). However, recognising the probability of traumatic lived experience, which people have survived, demands a more humane, caring and pro-active response to the person. Responses grounded in knowledge, respect and the interpersonal may enable the person to connect or reconnect with self and others. Data from both phases of the research suggests the importance of practical support, encouragement and effective liaison in supporting the person's connection with others and the world around them.

The importance of the practical, encouragement and effective liaison

Data from both phases of the project indicates the importance of broader social supports, which, evidence suggests, service users can prefer over more specialist professional interventions (Ikkos et al., 2011). MHSW is particularly suited to responding to such broader preferences, given that some have suggested that its function in mental health is to help clients cope with day-to-day tasks and to influence the 'social and physical environments to be more responsive to meeting their needs' (Rovinelli-Heller and Gittan, 2011, p 14). There is a focus on the person in their environment and support with services to meet *'common needs'* (Newhill and Korr, 2004, p 303). Indeed, research indicates that service users value the practical help offered by social workers (Lishman, 2009).

A majority of service users in Phase 1 of the project stress the importance of practical support, defined by them as relating to housing, benefit advice and help in getting out of the house. One service user described the long-lasting effects of such support, *'But yes, she helped me and she's actually helped me in a way that's stayed with me to this day really, helped me to go out because I refused to go outside my front door, because I was agoraphobic'* (20 June 2007). Similarly, a number of MHSWs in Phase 2 associate social work with the broader, more practical types of support, powerful tools which should not be *underestimated* as they can lead the MHSW to support the person in other ways and also help to renegotiate power differentials. However, one MHSW acknowledged how difficult it can now be for MHSWs to offer practical support, *'I think it's really important, but it's fallen by the wayside a bit because we were talking actually … there was a time when we did an awful lot of more practical stuff than we do now'* (25 May 2010).

Encouragement both in reality and as a motivator were important precursors for a number of service users in Phase 1. One participant (27 June 2007) described how the MHSW always seemed to be *'there … to encourage me to get out and do things'*. Whereas for four participants the MHSW can help them to develop themselves and look forward, as someone who encourages them, from whom they can learn even when they are not physically present. Data from Phase 2 similarly supports the importance of the MHSW *alongside* the person, in some instances quite literally:

> *I'll sit with them and say 'Go on, I'll sit with you while you make the call' and as we struggle with it, it might be 'OK, I'll dial', and they come back, come back, come back until we get something they can do and they succeed. So there's always that push towards them being competent, but it's always the support is there as well.*
>
> (Phase 2, 1 June 2010)

The data reaffirms, however, that support should be alongside the person rather than *doing it for them* (Phase 2, 13 April 2010).

Social work in its role of supporting the person in their environment (Rovinelli-Heller and Gittan, 2011) is associated with supporting the family and social network. This association is reflected in data from Phases 1 and 2. Service users described the importance of effective liaison which facilitated the involvement of others, such as occupational therapy or welfare rights officers. Efficacy appears to be associated with negotiation, as one service user describes how the MHSW liaises with her psychiatrist (Phase 1, 24 July 2007) and how her allocated MHSW communicates between her and her psychiatrist: *'She won't just go off and do it; she'll let me know'*. This participant knows that the MHSW will speak to the psychiatrist even if she herself does not want an appointment: *'She'd leave it. She'd just explain'* (24 July 2007). Interestingly, this theme is similarly picked up from data from Phase 2 when one MHSW describes how she will:

> go back and say, 'Remember what doctor so-and-so said to you? Go and give that a try and then maybe you can call me back if things like that haven't worked this afternoon' or something. So it's just to reinforce and keep that door of communication wide open all the time.
>
> (Phase 2, 13 April 2010)

However, data also highlights how interprofessional working can frequently be less than effective (Mangan et al., 2015), as one MHSW describes here, *'obviously you're relying on other agencies to do their bit and sometimes you're harassing other agencies to say "Well, this person hasn't seen their children in like x amount of time" – so it can be frustrating'* (Phase 2, 07 September 2011). It is apparent perhaps that differing priorities and core values (Mangan et al., 2015) contributed to the inefficacy of this interprofessional network, to the detriment of the person with personality disorder. This section has stressed the importance of practical support, encouragement and effective liaison to enhance connection and complement that derived from the relational security gained from more humane, caring and proactive responses to the person with personality disorder.

Conclusion

This chapter has set out my belief in the value of a social perspective on personality disorder, my motivations for the research project, the project's rationale, its theoretical foundations and methodology. A qualitative approach, interviewing both service users and MHSWs, has produced a grounded theory which suggests it is relevant to understand personality disorder as a response to traumatic experience, particularly in the early years. It suggests also the value of humane, empathic, prosocial relationships with service users and broad, social supports to empower the person's more constructive response to traumatic experience. The research findings indicate that personality disorder resists singular explanation, is more heterogeneous than discrete, which has consequences for professional understanding. Confused professional understandings of the disorder can contribute to distant and negative responses characterised by fear, resignation, denial and rejection, which only compound stigma, self-stigma, alienation and risk. Findings underline the importance of recognising the person with personality disorder as quite possibly a survivor of destructive and traumatic experience living with intense and overwhelming levels of innermost distress. We have established the importance of caring relational bonds, founded on the knowledge of the person and personality disorder, which can in turn enable the MHSW's professional use of self to evidence respect, listening and engagement with the person. Humane, prosocial relationships will enable broad social supports which together would support the person's connection or reconnection with self, others and the world around. The following chapter will consider those findings which suggest how MHSW practice in the area of personality disorder might be better informed.

Summary points

• A social perspective on personality disorder connects with current health and well-being agendas.

• A social perspective on personality disorder is founded on an understanding of trauma to inform humane, empathic relationships.

• It is important to reframe the person with personality disorder as a possible survivor of traumatic experience.

• The knowledge of the person and diagnosis is important to inspire the professional use of self.

• The importance of the relational to inspire broad social supports and promote the person's connection and/or reconnection with self, others and the world around them.

Taking it further

Castillo, H (2015) *The Reality of Recovery in Personality Disorder*. London: Jessica Kingsley.

Reiland, R (2004) *Get Me Out of Here: My Recovery from Borderline Personality Disorder*. Center City, MN: Hazelden Publishing.

5 Research findings: how practice might be better informed

Critical questions

» *How might we balance our knowledge and understanding of personality disorder more?*

» *What do we mean by citizenship?*

» *Can participation enhance citizenship?*

» *What are the key features of a better-informed practice?*

Introduction

By highlighting the relevance of experience, particularly trauma, the professional relationship and broad social supports in practice with people with personality disorder, we are in turn suggesting the importance of balance and equilibrium in the knowledge and understanding of the diagnosis. We have suggested that form should be balanced with content, subjective knowledge with objective and that the psychiatric, psychological and social should be utilised in complementary rather than competitive ways. Balancing our ways of understanding, and responding to the reality of personality disorder, is not only suited to modern, multidisciplinary mental health services, but might also help assure better outcomes for people with the diagnosis. We suggest a more balanced approach requires, first, a more articulate response from MHSW, to evidence the significance of MHSW's knowledge and role and, second, dialogue and negotiation between both mental health professionals and between mental health professionals and service users. However, the latter conversation raises questions about whether we perceive service users with personality disorder as citizens and, moreover, whether we respect their similar obligations, contributions, freedoms and rights as we respect our own (Jordan, 1975).

We suggested, in Chapter 3, the value of empowerment through active citizenship rather than market choice (Postle and Beresford, 2007). Active citizenship extends Marshall's

(1987) seminal work delineating universal political, social and civil rights, to embrace diversity and difference, including the right of participation (Lister, 2007). In Chapter 4 I set out my career-long commitment to the development of practice through collaboration with service users (Ramon et al., 2004). The project which underpins this book epitomises my commitment, particularly as the third research question asked service users and MHSWs how practice in the area of personality disorder might be better informed. Furthermore, MHSWs were asked to comment on service users' ideas about just how practice might be better informed. Both project and book therefore reflect my commitment to partnership, presenting the voices of those on the margins, particularly service users, with the aim of realising a practice more able to challenge the discrimination associated with personality disorder in mental health services and in society more generally (NIMHE, 2003; Tetley et al., 2012). Notwithstanding, the project presents, equally, a voice of MHSW which for some experiences a differential status, greater political pressure and more intense stigma than all of the other professions operating within modern mental health services (Bailey and Liyanage, 2012). This book therefore supports a more active conception of citizenship, with respect for the rights, obligations, freedoms and contributions of both service users with personality disorder and MHSWs (Jordan, 1975). This chapter will set out the findings from both phases of the research to suggest how MHSW practice may be better informed through understanding person and diagnosis; greater transparency and consistency; the provision of feedback; modelling; supporting the person's social and family network and practical support. However, as these findings spring from a project grounded in the participation of service users as partners with MHSWs, the chapter will first summarise the recent movement to improve public services through the involvement of service users as both consumers and producers of welfare services (Needham, 2007).

Citizenship and its meaning

Arnstein's (1969) ladder of citizen participation outlines eight rungs, from *participation* as citizen manipulation and therapy at the bottom, to participation as citizen control at the top. Here, the first rungs on the ladder describe '*levels of "non-participation" that possibly, for some substitute for genuine participation*' (ibid., p 217). Citizen control, on the contrary, guarantees citizen governance, management and powers of negotiation (ibid.). Although some have critiqued Arnstein's typology as being too orientated to power (Tritter and McCallum, 2006), it offers a starting point for a consideration of the movement in the UK to improve health and social care services through public participation and involvement (ibid.). However, a rush to understand the advancement of service provision through participation can obscure inherent tensions, not the least of which surround the political meanings of citizen, and citizenship as both an inclusionary and exclusionary force (Lister, 2007). It is beyond the scope of this chapter, indeed the book, to analyse the contested nature of citizen and citizenship in any real depth. However, we would like to offer a cursory consideration to gain an insight into the degree to which service development, in the UK, has been based on the involvement of the public as passive consumers or active citizens (Barnes et al., 1999; Lister, 1998).

Citizenship is as we have suggested an oblique concept, with its roots, as Lister (2007) suggests, in two different political traditions, the liberal and the republican. Whereas the former emphasises the individual, the latter accentuates the community and individual obligations to that community (ibid.). Citizenship is perhaps more than the acquisition of civil, political and social rights (Marshall, 1987); it is about the ability to participate as active citizens in the governance and management of institutions and organisations within our communities in order to ensure greater equality and social justice for all (Pahl, 1990). This is not to suggest that citizenship is solely dependent on action (Lister, 2007). Although we realise the need for rational, self-contained individuals in a productive Western economy (Geertz, 1997), we have suggested that an over-reliance on the technical, bounded and rational individual marginal-ises the social and the relational, with significant implications for society and its institutions including social work. Citizenship is not removed from such implications.

As an essentially universal concept (Marshall, 1987), citizenship can exclude those who are unable to meet society's expectations for exacting, self-contained individuals. Citizenship for *them* can only ever be partial. Moreover, we saw in Chapter 4 how we can split *good* from *bad*, *us* from *them*, individually and socially, through a process of Othering (Klein, 1959). Citizens who do not meet society's expectations are split off as non-citizens or perhaps less than human (Young, 1999). Evidence certainly suggests that people with personality disor-der have been designated as the demonised Other, which induces only partial understand-ings and therefore compounds risk and alienation (NIMHE, 2003; Wright et al., 2007). We support Lister's (2007) argument that citizenship is both a matter of rights *and* participation, which, as agent individuals, we are able to exercise. However, our opportunities for develop-ment and our abilities to take responsibility for this process (Alexander and Mohanty, 1997) are differential. Self and agency are, we would suggest, products of the social contexts in which they are embedded (Rose, 1986; Sampson, 2003). Rights, of participation for exam-ple, can counteract those contexts which limit abilities to determine self, identity and agency and thereby enable more active citizenship (Postle and Beresford, 2007).

The research at the heart of this book invited people with personality disorder, and MHSWs to participate in a project to inform our understanding of diagnosis and practice. Although it may be far from the top rung of the citizen participation ladder, the research bridged the worlds of both service users as citizens and MHSWs, who may be perceived as the *powerhold-ers* (Arnstein, 1969). In this sense I, as the researcher, acted as the negotiator attempting to realise some appreciation of how personality disorder and MHSW may be better informed and understood. There is the question, of course, of how much I trust myself, or others, to act on these findings (Guba and Lincoln, 1985). Although the findings are representative neither of all service users with personality disorder nor all MHSWs, the research exemplifies fairness, ontological and educative authenticity both in process and execution (ibid.). First, the voices of all participants, whether agreeing or contradicting, were included. Second, data reveals how the research questions encouraged participants to reflect anew on the nature of personality disorder and MHSW practice. Data specific to the third research question reveals how MHSWs came '*to appreciate (apprehend, discern, understand) – not necessarily like or agree with – the constructions that are made by others and to understand how those constructions are rooted in the different value systems of those others*' (Guba and Lincoln, 1986, cited in Guba and Lincoln, 1989, pp 248–49). For example, one participant from Phase 2 responds to service users' ideas about how MHSWs need to understand the person and the diagnosis. The initial response seems to doubt whether MHSWs need to understand the diagnosis, but then the participant thinks again and says:

> *Yeah, I can understand that because it has been used as quite a denigrating term, and yet if you've actually been diagnosed you might not feel it's the stigma – you might just be relieved that somebody's sort of given a name to this chaos that you're caught up in, and so they can have very positive feelings about it, so yeah, I can understand that.*
>
> (4 May 2010)

Third, the project's grounded theory evidences originality; it emerged from a saturated data set and was produced through a constant comparative method (Glaser and Strauss, 1967). Given the authenticity of process and findings, we would suggest that the data from this project can be relied upon for future action. Moreover, the project valued the participation of people with personality disorder as active citizens, in an attempt to ensure MHSW practice is more responsive to the ideas of some of the people who use its services. Clearly, the project and I as the researcher have been influenced by the growth of public participation and involvement in health and social care services over the course of the past three decades (Needham, 2007).

Public participation and involvement

Public involvement in the design, delivery and implementation of health and social care services has grown out of a dissatisfaction with seemingly unresponsive, provider-centric services (Bovaird, 2007; Bruch, 2002). Policy, service development and management is now not simply the preserve of qualified professionals, but much more a matter of negotiation between users and providers of services as co-producers (Alford, 1998). Co-production centres on different contributions to a good or service of value to themselves and others (Ostrom, 1996; Ramirez, 1999). Questions arise, however, around the extent of these contributions and whether they are made in equal measure (Bovaird, 2007). Bovaird defines co-production as '*the provision of services through regular, long-term relationships between professionalised service providers (in any sector) and service users or other members of the community where all parties make substantial resource contributions*' (ibid., p 847). Tritter and McCallum (2006) argue that while UK health and social care services have sought the involvement of both patients and service users, this has been within a context of liberal, marketised relations (DoH, 1990), where the former has express rights to choose as consumers. Involvement becomes an expression of choice and a mechanism for provider feedback rather than the exercise of citizen control as co-producers. As Longley (1996) suggests, '*the preference for consumerism and individual choice is more about customer relations than any enhanced rights which entail true partnership or power sharing*' (p 147).

A model of participation which recognises that we are more than consumers, that we are also producers of public services (Alford, 1998), emphasises our interdependency as service users, professionals, carers and employees (Ostrom, 1996). Unsurprisingly perhaps, co-production is a contested concept, with models ranging from the individual (Brudney and England, 1983) to the collective (Needham, 2007). Some suggest that co-production occurs on a continuum between high levels of professional/low levels of user input on the one end, with high levels of user/low levels of professional input on the other (Miller and Stirling, 2004). Needham (2007) suggests that zero sum forms of co-production substitute user participation for that of professionals, whereas in positive sum approaches professionals and users occupy complementary roles in the co-production of services (Wirth, 1991). Positive sum approaches resonate with the research for this book, as although not an example of co-production, the project underlines the importance of interdependence, interaction and dialogue, where *'users and providers can discuss service provision away from the point of delivery'* (Needham, 2007, p 225). Although this was a vicarious process, both samples participated with full knowledge of the research design, in that I as the researcher would ask MHSW participants for feedback on service users' ideas about how MHSW practice might be better informed.

Co-production, particularly in its positive sum guise, it must be said, raises anxieties and accentuates service users' responsibilities for risk (Ostrom, 1996). However, it emphasises the importance of otherwise marginalised voices, those of service users and frontline practitioners, such as MHSWs, for a more responsive service (Bailey and Liyanage, 2012). Research, carried out by Needham in 2006, brought housing officers and tenants together in the same workshop. Interesting parallels with social work are evident: the desire for a more personalised service, user frustrations with providers, ie housing officers, a gulf in perceptions between providers and users exemplified by false provider perceptions about rising user expectations and false user assumptions about provider indifference. Although challenging, the process of bringing users and providers together in this way ultimately helped to identify *'shared priorities'* and the benefits of *'dialogue between co-producers'* for *'more effective engagement at the point of delivery'* (Needham, 2007, p 228).

We saw in Chapter 4 how relationships between service users with personality disorder and mental health professionals and providers can be fraught with frustration, distance and negative responses. Stalker et al. (2005) revealed how an inconsistency in provision can undermine trust in and efficacy of the user/provider relationship. Furthermore, Irvine (1996) shows how the unrealistic expectations of social work staff, held by both users and fellow providers, can leave social workers feeling isolated and alone in their work with people with personality disorder. Data from this project, detailed in Chapter 4, revealed the unhelpful consequences of such processes, the mutual construction of service users and MHSWs as the *Other* (Klein, 1959). However, Chapter 4 also revealed the beginnings of commonalities between service users and MHSWs, particularly around the relevance of trauma to understanding the diagnosis, the intensity of distress and the importance of support which emphasises care and helps the person to connect or reconnect with self, others and the world around them.

As the researcher, I make no claims for co-production. As the sole researcher, I was responsible for the idea, design and implementation of the project and its methods. However, we do suggest that the project shares some similarities, in principle, with more positive sum co-production approaches, namely the recognition of user/provider interdependence and the importance of dialogue between users and providers. Whereas the conversation between users and MHSWs was only vicarious, through me as the researcher, the fieldwork for Phases 1 and 2 occurred consecutively and moreover provided an opportunity to investigate how MHSW practice may be better informed. Service users were asked for their thoughts on *'how*

MHSW practice could be different for people with personality disorder'. MHSWs in Phase 2 were then asked to comment on service users' ideas. This chapter will now present those findings which suggest that MHSW practice may be better informed by understanding person and diagnosis; greater transparency and consistency; the provision of feedback; modelling; supporting the person's social and family network and practical support.

Understanding person and diagnosis

Service users in Phase 1 suggested the importance of MHSWs understanding both person and diagnosis for better-informed practice. Three service users emphasised the importance of the MHSW understanding the person, and five emphasised the importance of the MHSW understanding the diagnosis. One participant described how MHSWs need to:

> *be in tune with that person, they have got to get to know that person's needs and what that person needs to move on, not just push them to one side. Understand that person's needs because personality disorder comes under a very broad umbrella and everybody has got a different personality part of their disorder, and you've got to know that person before you can help that person and support that person.*
>
> (Phase 1, 09 January 2008)

Another suggests that *'more understanding'*, crucially of *'what you're going through'* (Phase 1, 20 April 2007) is vitally important. Seeing the person and appreciating their life history might help avoid stereotypical responses and thereby encourage a more humane and effective response to the person with personality disorder. However, five participants also stressed the need for MHSWs to understand the diagnosis. As one suggests, here, more training in personality disorder is required, *'when mental health social workers do their training they should do more training on personality disorder ... so they've got more understanding of the diagnosis, because I don't think social workers fully understand personality disorders... if the social worker doesn't understand your diagnosis then they're no good to you'* (Phase 1, 09 January 2007). The value some service users attached to MHSWs understanding the diagnosis was a little unexpected. However, if the experience of trauma disconnects the person from everything around them, including self, the diagnosis is possibly the only route for acquiring an identity (Read et al., 2006). Confidence in the MHSW therefore becomes ever more essential as it enables them to engage with the nature of the person's distress. If practice is based on perceptions (Luborsky, 1984) and attitudes (Downie, 2011, pp 23–35) as well as interventions, a confident, credible MHSW could well be important.

MHSWs were consequently asked to comment in Phase 2 on the importance of MHSWs understanding both person and diagnosis. Intriguingly, while MHSWs agreed on the importance of both, priorities differed from service users. The majority, nine MHSWs, believed that understanding the person was more important for them than understanding the diagnosis. As one participant (Phase 2, 07 November 2011) suggested, *'it is very important to understand the person just as much as the diagnosis, because at the end of the day the diagnosis has come from what has happened to the person through their life, so you've got to kind of understand the bare bones of somebody to understand everything that's gone on and what's made them what they are'*. Interestingly, in this sample, MHSWs' commitment to the person, utilising the person's experience as a lens on the present is reaffirmed (Rovinelli-Heller and Gittan, 2011). The emphasis on the person in Phase 2 might also illuminate MHSW's long-standing and ambivalent relationship with systems of diagnostic classification, in that they are important only for how much they tell us about how the person lives with the diagnosis and how it changes their world (Kvaternik and Grebenc, 2009). Intriguingly, three MHSWs did find some value in the diagnosis and systems of classification, indicating how they can inform an approach to the person.

The findings of this project reveal some shared appreciation about how practice may be better informed through MHSWs gaining greater understanding of the person and the diagnosis. However, the different priorities of service users and MHSWs need to be kept in mind. Some service users prioritised MHSWs' understanding of the diagnosis over and above the person. This may reflect their need for confidence in the mental health professional. In lives possibly characterised by chaos and disconnection, a solid and meaningful presence can be vital (Bussey and Wise, 2007). The priority that some MHSWs in Phase 2 showed to understanding the person complements some of the service users' ideas. However, it may also reflect the profession's ambivalent relationship with psychiatric classification systems. The commitment of these MHSWs to the person reaffirms the profession's obligation to first person narratives which communicate the impact of their experience on them as people (BASW, 2015; Rovinelli-Heller and Gittan, 2011). We would suggest that a MHSW's understanding of the person, confident in their knowledge of the diagnosis, may help to realise a more humane and effective response to service users with personality disorder. Some service users suggested how greater transparency and consistency would also help realise a different, more informed practice.

Transparency and consistency

Evidence suggests that the reality of social work intervention and practice, in whatever area, frequently relies on incomplete, conflicting and/or inaccurate information (Bortoli and Dolan, 2015). Despite this, transparency is the goal of new public management and evidence-based practice which is required in organisational, legal and practice contexts and in decision making (ibid.; Buckley et al., 2011). Transparent accountability to policy can increase public esteem in social work (Pollock, 2014). Notwithstanding this, evidence suggests that service users remain dissatisfied with the information available to them and moreover the information written about them (Buckley et al., 2011). Transparency of information and decision making is a feature of better-informed relationships between service users and social workers, which in turn can help compensate for the harsher aspects and consequences of social work intervention (ibid.). Consistency in service provision and in our interaction with service users and carers would appear to some extent as an associated feature of better-informed relationships. Evidence suggests, however, that high staff turnover, seemingly related to stress and deficits in environments for staff, can have a material impact on social work practice (Munroe and Hubbard, 2011). Although evidence suggests that social workers struggle consistently with certain aspects of our more technical and rational practice (Broadhurst et al., 2010), we do not always provide a consistent service to service users, which has implications for the quality of the relationship and ultimately the efficacy of outcomes for service users and carers.

Findings from Phase 1 of this project certainly suggest that MHSW practice would be better informed through greater transparency of information and consistency of service. One participant described how consistency is required because people *'need to get on with their lives. They have other things to do'* (Phase 1, 10 July 2007). This participant goes on to describe her frustrations with being left to wait for social workers who are late, or being thrown completely when a new worker was allocated to her *case*, without any prior information that this was going to happen. Another participant reveals an inconsistency and therefore lack of transparency about what was said to him, and what he suspects was actually thought about him:

> *I think they were kind of ... I think they were a bit prejudiced in a way. I kinda think they had their own notion. Maybe they thought I was untreatable, maybe they believed in their head that I was untreatable, that's what they would have said in their meetings... but they didn't say that to me.*
>
> (Phase 1, 09 January 2007)

When MHSWs were asked to comment on greater transparency and consistency as a possible feature of better-informed practice with people with personality disorder, participants agreed on both it being fundamental to practice and to being fair with service users. However, the data from Phase 2 indicates that neither transparency nor consistency is *'simple goods'* (Phase 2, 01 December 2010). Some MHSWs suggested that to aim for consistency, in an inconsistent world, raises false expectations about life, with which service users will *'have to cope'* (Phase 2, 01 December 2010). It is evident that for the MHSWs sampled, the profession's ability to maintain transparency and consistency in practice is dependent on different contexts and expectations. One participant describes how transparency can be inhibited:

> *Yeah, yeah, well I think we do have a need to be transparent, we need to be honest, and I think quite often, yep, I put my hands up, not really honest with the person, you know sometimes I feel like saying I'm really stuck here, come on, can you help me out, because I don't want them to feel that 'Oh well, if you don't know what do to, I'm the person that's suffering. What do you think I'm going to feel like if you tell me that'?*
>
> (Phase 2, 18 May 2010)

In some respects this comment takes us back to the need for confident, meaningful structures in a world of chaos and disconnection (Bussey and Wise, 2007). While the type of disclosure this participant imagines here may threaten her conception of professional credibility, such transparency may actually promote dialogue and understanding about the person's experience, needs and strengths (Glicken, 2004). Dialogue-based partnerships can encourage the reformulation of problems and bring about positive change (Livesley, 2003). Furthermore, while people with personality disorder do ultimately have to cope with the inconsistencies of others around them, supportive relationships that promote consistency and transparency may be a mechanism through which they can learn to cope (Livesley, 2003). Interestingly, three MHSWs suggested the importance of transparency and consistency with colleagues, as one participant indicates here, *'so that we all sing from the same hymn sheet, essentially, so that the approach to this individual is consistent'* (Phase 2, 24 November 2010). This statement appears to reflect the value of a team approach to personality disorder founded on effective communication and support, enabling staff to respond to the person and their family, if appropriate, in a consistent manner, with time for staff to reflect with and validate the person (McNee et al., 2014).

The importance attached to transparency and consistency reflects expectations that mental health professionals will maintain appropriate relationships and be honest (Bhugra, 2008). We would suggest therefore that greater transparency and consistency would better inform MHSW practice in the area of personality disorder. Given the latter's relationship to traumatic experience, transparency and consistency appear particularly relevant. Whether the consequences of trauma are defined as deficits (Livesley, 2003) or losses of the gravest kind (Estroff, 1989), the person's conception of self and ability to engage in relationships can be profoundly affected (Erikson, 1968). In a world that is chaotic, disorganised and unpredictable the importance of consistency and transparency should not be underestimated. However, different contexts of practice and expectations of service users, colleagues and fellow professionals have to be kept in mind. Neither transparency nor consistency is simple goods which can make both *tricky* (Phase 2, 25 May 2010) to operationalise in practice. Feedback, as another feature of honest practice (Bhugra, 2008), was also identified by service users as an attribute of better-informed MHSW practice with people with personality disorder.

Feedback and dialogue is important

Social work requires more than the delivery of an accountable, transparent and consistent service. It requires the professional use of self to establish supportive relationships and intervention where circumstances may be morally problematic (Clark, 2007). Feedback as a mechanism for helping people negotiate complex and/or problematic situations may be regarded as an element of good practice, related to honesty, openness and perhaps *modern* or *new* professionalism (Stern, 2004). Five participants in Phase 1 described how feedback from the MHSW could better inform practice in the area of personality disorder. Data suggests how such feedback could be individual or collective, with the aim of validating thoughts and feelings or could be more constructively critical to help the person *self-develop* (Phase 1, 20 June 2007). Two participants suggested the need for more dialogue between service users with personality disorder, MHSWs and all mental health professionals, '*they need to be in a panel, we need to have a panel of people with mental health, with PD, to ask questions, for them to be on the spot. Not to be humiliated or to be subjected to ridicule, but to have a discussion on what they can see could improve the way they move forward*' (Phase 1, 09 January 2008).

Reflective perhaps of a positive sum approach to the co-production of services (Wirth, 1991), these ideas highlight the importance of feedback for learning and personal development especially when patterns of behaviour or functioning are well established (Westberg and Jason, 2001). People who have experienced trauma in their early lives, especially from caregivers, may never have had an opportunity to receive constructive feedback on their thoughts, feelings and behaviours. It is possible that invalidating thoughts, feelings and behaviours can take hold. We would suggest that feedback, as a feature of effective relationships (Wood et al., 2010), can challenge that which invalidates the person and their relationships (Cherry, 2005). Moreover, feedback can contribute positively to the person's motivation, levels of social support, coping skills (Wood et al., 2010) and to their personal recovery, or more prosaically, to their '*becoming new*' (Deegan, 2001, p 18; Castillo, 2010).

MHSWs similarly defined feedback as positive and constructively critical but also suggested that feedback should include comment on what they, as the MHSW, had been able to achieve or not, on the service user's behalf. Some MHSWs agreed that feedback could be an important mechanism for helping the person to move on or *self-develop* (Phase 1, 20 April 2007). As one participant describes:

> *how else are people going to know, because you can't remember sometimes how you were feeling a week ago and what was going on, so unless the person that's working alongside you in these things actually can sometimes say, 'Well actually I recall a week ago, and things were very different, and look what you've done – do you think that's been helpful?' and sort of help that person reflect; if you don't give that feedback, they've got nothing to go on.*

(Phase 2, 13 April 2010)

However, data from Phase 2 also indicates a need for the appreciation of the different contexts and complexities of MHSW practice. Some MHSWs reflected on how feedback, both positive and constructively critical, requires skill, patience and time. Time can be lacking in the context of practice in modern, mental health services under increasing resource pressure (BBC, 2015). Genuine feedback may not be possible in services based on '*rush, rush, rush*', and if not genuine, service users can '*feel fobbed off and that their problems are minimised*' (Phase 2, 01 December 2010). Moreover, deficits in skills, or the perception of it, can risk patronising service users, as three participants describe, '*to do it [feedback] properly is quite a skill*' (BS), '*you can come across as being really patronising*' (Phase 2, 16 March 2010 and 13 April 2010).

The data indicates some MHSW agreement about how the provision of feedback might better inform practice with people with personality disorder. However, feedback, as with transparency and consistency, needs to be set within the contexts and complexities of MHSW practice. Context is vital and can indeed determine the efficacy of feedback; and time and skill is important too. We suggested in Chapter 3 that a relational style of management befits the social work task and the unpredictability of human beings as its core business (Ruch, 2012). Relational management styles, which valorise the social and the power of the professional relationship, could also appreciate the value of time, both for change and for effective support and intervention. Data from Phase 2 also indicates a need for investment in MHSW education and training to help ensure the delivery of effective feedback. Investment would be completely justifiable as evidence suggests that social work involvement in sensitive, interpersonal interaction, advocacy and *educational* assistance can enhance service users' social capital, with beneficial effects for their physical and psychological well-being (McLeod et al., 2008). We would suggest that feedback, delivered with time and skill, could be an important feature of better-informed MHSW practice. However, some have suggested that a person's ability to assimilate feedback is in part dependent on the availability of appropriate role models (Westberg and Jason, 2001). It is perhaps no surprise therefore that service users in Phase 1 saw the value of MHSWs as models offering a '*bit more reality*' (Phase 1, 20 June 2007) in their lives.

Modelling

Modelling has been long associated with social work intervention in problematic issues impacting on peoples' lives. As Clark (2006) suggests, the profession has a pedagogical role, the expectation to teach '*standards of good conduct, social responsibility and community values*' (p 81). This raises questions about the profession's worthiness for such a role and the virtues of individual workers. A good example is perhaps not best set by immoral standards or a questionable lifestyle (Carr, 1991). However, virtues of prudence, perception, justice and bravery can be acquired and developed by social work education and training (McBeath and Webb, 2002). The latter suggests that it is through a commitment to both intellectual and practical values that social workers achieve a '*moral and social richness of understanding*' with service users (p 1033). Data from both phases of this research project points to social work's history of modelling and the relevance of MHSWs' capacity to model and inspire service users, but also raises questions about the *virtues* of the profession which can possibly undermine MHSWs' capacity to model.

Three service users in Phase 1 suggested that MHSWs possess the capacity to model and inspire, as one describes here, being '*a consistent solid person who is not going to rescue you or anything or necessarily be brilliant when you are sobbing or whatever, but just that kind of giving you, if you don't have it yourself, giving you an experience of what it could be like to lead a normal life almost by example*' (20 June 2007). Nothing special, just a person with a '*a sense of who they are very much somebody who is in the world, understands the world, is comfortable in the world; they are a consistent presence*' (ibid.). Six MHSWs in Phase 2 agreed that modelling is one of our '*tools of the trade*' (Phase 2, 18 May 2010). Moreover, modelling within the space offered by an effective professional relationship gives an opportunity to the person '*to try out new, different ways of relating, it is really important*' (Phase 2, 01 December 2010). Another participant described modelling as '*one of the ways in which a social worker can work with people is just really to be there, role modelling, something like that*' (Phase 2, 14 April 2010).

However, some MHSWs questioned social workers' capacity, indeed virtues, for modelling, suggesting that there is nothing unique or *superhuman* about social workers to make them '*uniquely capable individuals living a straightforward life in a complicated world*' (Phase 2, 12 May 2007). Another participant suggested that the capacity to model is not exclusive to social workers and moreover that differential lived experience can compromise the capacity to model, '*it's part of the normalising, I think. It's difficult, isn't it, because we're all different ages and things so I am not sure entirely, yeah, I guess everything you're doing is sort of modelling how to a look at a problem for instance, and how to manage feelings and being honest about*' (Phase 2, 04 May 2010).

Data from both phases suggests a relationship between feedback and modelling similar to prosocial modelling (Trotter, 2004), a feature of prosocial practice (Cherry, 2005, 2010). Pro social practice has been seen to be effective in many fields where the person is involuntary or hard to engage. It has been particularly effective in encouraging validating, prosocial thoughts and behaviours in work with offenders and within child protection settings (Trotter, 2004). Prosocial modelling relies on openness and clarity about roles, expectations and boundaries (ibid.). Any fallibility, as social workers and people, should not necessarily be an issue as the worker should take every opportunity, even when mistakes are made, to model prosocial behaviour through an empathic, professional relationship or partnership (Cherry, 2005). If professional virtues are acquired through a continuous process of lifelong learning, social workers should be as capable of learning from mistakes as anyone else (McBeath and Webb, 2002). Open, transparent, consistent relationships, which employ feedback and modelling, offer opportunities to reinforce validating thoughts and behaviours while challenging those invalidating ones. This might involve some risk for some mental health professionals, including MHSWs, as it calls for a different way of thinking: not *'I can't apologise because this person will manipulate it'*, but *'I've made a mistake; this person is a person and as such deserves an apology. We may both learn from their reaction to my apology'*. Indeed, modelling which highlights caring attitudes and bonds can restate professionalism (Downie, 2011, pp 23–35) rather than compromise it. There is the issue of who defines what *prosocial* behaviour is, but data from this project indicates that prosocial modelling may have relevance in working with personality disorder.

We have seen how data relevant to the question of how MHSW practice might be better informed suggests agreement on the importance of understanding person and diagnosis, greater transparency and consistency and the use of feedback and modelling. However, different practice contexts and complexities have to be accounted for. The evident similarities to Cherry's conception of prosocial practice (2010) appears to underline the value of these findings for MHSW practice with people with personality disorder. Personality disorder's relationship to early traumatic experience and the intensity of distress can make trust difficult and people difficult to engage (NIMHE, 2003). However, transparent and consistent, prosocial relationships based on knowledge, strengths, employing feedback and modelling offer opportunities to validate the person and moreover challenge their invalidating thoughts, feelings and behaviour. For those who may never have the opportunity to evaluate themselves in relation to others or to receive constructive feedback, a professional relationship offering attributes such as these may be invaluable for the person and therefore contribute to more positive connections with self, others and the world around them. We have noted at times the consequences personality disorder can have for the person's relationships with family and friends, the difficulties in maintaining and retaining these relationships, relationships which can positively contribute to recovery (Biegel et al., 2013). The next section will set out MHSW's response to service users' ideas about how MHSW support for the person's family and social network might better inform MHSW practice.

Support for the person's family and social network

Social work has long been associated with supporting social and family networks (Rovinelli-Heller and Gittan, 2011). Evidence suggests that high-quality intensive interventions with families can be effective (Forrester et al., 2016). The support of close family and friends through high-quality relationships can be vital for the person's ongoing recovery from mental disorder (Biegel et al., 2013). Service user participants in Phase 1 highlighted the importance of support for the person's family. One participant described how such support could be an indicator of the MHSW's trust in that network, 'they know that when you're speaking to them, the other people they get support from, whether it's family, friends or places like this that you trust them enough to actually then be speaking to them as well' (Phase 1, 24 July 2007). Another service user described how a lack of social work support for her daughter, at the height of the participant's illness, had and continues to have far-reaching implications as her daughter continues to 'wonder whether she'll get the same sort of problems as what her mum's got. And that can be a worry, can't it? For any children, I suppose, but when a mum or dad has got that, "Am I going to get that?"' (Phase 1, 24 July 2007). Consequently this participant was, at the time of the interview, seeking support with rehousing, partly because her daughter, now an adult, struggles to return to the house in which she grew up and where her mother still lives.

MHSWs in Phase 2 agreed in principle with the idea that MHSWs should support the person's family and social network. Certainly, some suggested that such support is a crucial part of the MHSW role,

> in terms of maintaining those family relationships, because quite often someone with a personality disorder may reject those closest to them ... so I think it's important to have that, to be that link and to maintain that contact and to have that relationship and that transparency with the family members as much as with the service user.
>
> (Phase 2, 24 November 2010)

However, others suggested that such support could be *tricky* and very context dependent, as MHSWs can often find themselves 'working in the dark':

> I just feel and sometimes I get to the bottom of what happened there, sometimes I do ... Families have secrets they don't want us to know about. Sometimes I'm working in the dark really, I don't know the key, and I don't get in there.
>
> (Phase 2, 18 May 2010)

Other MHSWs described their concerns about a perceived lack of organisational support for MHSWs to engage in family work, particular challenges in maintaining confidentiality and the different experiences and expectations between the person and their network as one MHSW describes here, 'helping people work out how they want those relationships to be, and sometimes comment on what was healthy and what didn't feel so healthy, and enable them to reflect on what might be happening' (Phase 2, 04 May 2010). One participant saw supporting the person's family and social network very much as a double-edged sword, which can make the MHSW's life easier on the one hand and more complicated on the other, 'it makes my life so much easier if we can maintain family involvement. But we are often talking about parents that have been abusive' (Phase 2, 24 November 2010). Support for family and members of the person's social network would be fraught with challenges for the MHSW. However, such assistance appears to hold some significance, not the least to support carers with the challenges they can face and to ameliorate the risk of them neglecting their own mental health needs, emotional and physical general well-being (The Guardian, 2013). The rationale for MHSWs supporting the person's family and social network becomes more persuasive when we appreciate the impact of secondary traumatic stress on those close to the traumatised person (Bussey and Wise, 2007).

The complexity of the MHSW task is evident, as is the need to balance more than one perspective in the same context (Renouf and Bland, 2005; Ryan et al., 2005). However, the findings reaffirm the need for an empathic relationship that conveys genuine interest in the person and their lived experience (Cherry, 2010; Nathan and Webber, 2010) through the MHSW asking the right questions. Empowering the person's more constructive response to trauma is not possible in an environment of secrecy and avoidance (Bussey and Wise, 2007). The enormity of the task at times cannot be underestimated; the work is very dependent on context, and the MHSW would need to be supported in this work. However, such work may inform practice and MHSW's contribution in this area as well as supporting the person's connection or reconnection with others (Herman, 1992). Service users identified one final attribute of a better-informed MHSW practice: practical support.

The value of practical support

Three service users (F, A, S) suggested that practice would be better informed by more practical support and by the MHSW working alongside the service user. Service users described how '*being helped to get out in society more*' is important (Phase 1, 20 April 2010). Another (Phase 1, 20 June 2010) offered concrete suggestions about being supported, '*going to the supermarket, getting on a bus, any of these practical things is the issue, and they are very practical ways that the social worker could help*'. In response, some MHSWs agreed on the value of working with the person in practical ways. Indeed, one participant reported that he increasingly worked in this way, '*I'm no longer trying to change people, I'm trying to help individuals cope with what happens in their life ... now it's more about enhancing the capabilities that are under there, that are more helpful*' (Phase 2, 12 May 2010). This data reflects literature which suggests that service users with mental health problems want practical as well as emotional support from social workers (Beresford, 2012). It also reflects that literature which suggests how working with the person in their own environment can help to negotiate power differentials by illuminating a horizontal power-together approach rather than vertical power-over (Tew, 2006). Home visits and direct or support worker's practical support can promote the co-operative use of power and shared understandings from which more collaborative relationships may evolve (Wilson and Daly, 2007). However, one MHSW cautioned that MHSW's ability to support the person in more practical ways has '*fallen by the wayside*' (Phase 2, 25 May 2010).

Until now this chapter has considered MHSWs' responses to service users' ideas about how practice in the area of personality disorder may be better informed. However, data from Phase 2 revealed for some participants the value of service users as co-facilitators of social work training and education in personality disorder.

Service user involvement in education and training

The value base, policy context and professional standards of social work mean that the profession is adept at involving service users in the education and training of practitioners.

Moreover, Irvine, Molyneux and Gillman (2014) found that social work students report the experience as overwhelmingly positive and one that can have a direct bearing on their own practice. While issues of capacity would have to be addressed (Brown and Young, 2008), findings from Phase 2 of this project suggest the potential value of service users with personality disorder being involved as co-facilitators of social work education and training. The data substantiates a need for specialised training (Bowers, 2002; Duggan, 2007; NIMHE, 2003) with five MHSWs suggesting that this should involve service users, *'really good training would be quite good for social workers, and quality training, because sometimes it's not been good, not necessarily with the personality disorder but with other aspects, and I think actually service users being part of the training would be really good, to actually hear from them what it's like'* (Phase 2, 25 May 2010).

These findings reflect calls for further education in this area (Bateman and Fonagy, 2004; Cleary et al., 2002), an interest in the service-user perspective and the importance of understanding their lived experience and knowledge (Beresford, 2005; Nathan and Webber, 2010). Knowledge *'based on direct experience of policy and provision from the receiving end'* (Beresford, 2005, p 40) is an important source of expertise (Lester and Glasby, 2006). User involvement is meaningful because students remember the person's narrative (Repper and Breeze, 2007) and because it highlights our commonality and shared humanity (Simon, 2007, p 320). Balen et al. (2010) also found that qualifying students, including social work students, evaluated such training positively because it added value (p 416), helping them to understand the person's lived experience. While a post-course evaluation of training for qualified mental health professionals involving service users with personality disorder showed a drop in interest towards clients, it revealed increased understanding and skills and decreased pessimism and frustration (Castillo, 2011). However, organisational and practitioner support would be required in order to make the most of such involvement, as without commitment to practical arrangements, the emotional labour of service users and respect for the alternative epistemologies of experts by experience (Beresford and Branfield, 2006), involvement would appear tokenistic (Beresford and Croft, 2001).

Practice sensitive to the knowledge and experience of service users might encourage professional optimism, as such knowledge can *'challenge traditional assumptions and highlight key priorities that users would like to see addressed'* (Lester and Glasby, 2006, p 166). This is particularly relevant to the plight of people with personality disorder (NIMHE, 2003) facing therapeutic pessimism and inertia (Wright et al., 2007). These findings also raise a question about how far MHSW accepts medical notions of mental illness (Beresford, 2005), as these particular participants showed a positive interest in what the service user with personality disorder can contribute to the training and knowledge base of MHSW. The findings highlight the value of a social perspective on the diagnosis and a prosocial approach to the person. It is important, therefore, for training to reflect a social approach to both (Houston et al., 2005) the understanding and the enhancement of MHSW skills. As one MHSW reflected,

> *I would offer, not that complex, I think – and this is where within our services we get it wrong – because often they offer very dry training, very academic training, and it doesn't explain, it doesn't help a care coordinator to actually start to have some empathy with these people or even begin to like them. And that's what I want to do,*

and I want to start at the beginning, more basic, because ... we really do need the basic stuff. The basic stuff, such as for someone with personality disorder, cancelling a visit is catastrophic to them, that's when they'll self-harm because you let them down like everyone else ... training to help practitioners to understand why people get diagnosed with personality disorder, that these people aren't born like this, that these people have had traumatic pasts. I would like training that looks at attachment to help them understand that.

(Phase 2, 24 November 2010)

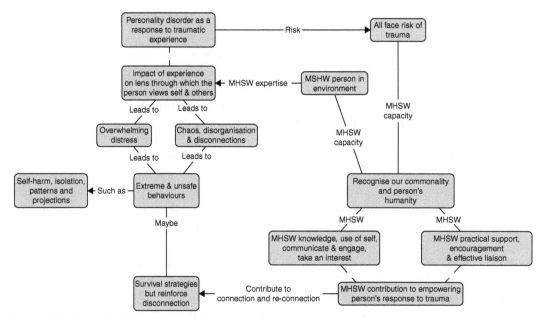

Figure 5.1 How MHSW practice in this area could be better informed.

Conclusion

Reflecting on the research findings from a project which emphasised the importance of dialogue and negotiation, especially with service users with personality disorder, this chapter has hopefully reaffirmed an important theme of this book: the need for balance and equilibrium in our understanding of and response to personality disorder. Although no claims for co-production are made, the experiences, thoughts and ideas of both service users and MHSWs were retrieved so that MHSW practice may be mutually informed. The project was reliant on the participation of service users and MHSWs. In some ways therefore the project and its findings underlines participation, where rights, obligations, freedoms and contributions are respected and hence conveys a more active citizenship, to which attention to fairness, in every aspect, ontological and educational authenticity can only add. Moreover, the research produced an original grounded theory which emerged from a saturated data set by means of a constant comparative method.

We have seen how practice, in the area of personality disorder, might be better informed by MHSW evidencing an informed understanding of both the person and diagnosis. While MHSWs may attach greater importance to the former, for a number of reasons, the latter should not be discounted, as a confident understanding of personality disorder may enable service user confidence in the MHSW. While different contexts and expectations have to be accounted for, greater transparency and consistency are important features of a better-informed practice. Neither are '*simple goods*' but both can promote dialogue and therefore greater understanding of experience, needs and strengths. It is possible that greater transparency and consistency in practice may help to ameliorate certain implications of some of the harsher consequences of social work intervention. Key attributes of prosocial practice featured prominently, namely feedback and modelling. Interestingly, both are seemingly interdependent as learning and personal development tools and very relevant given social work's historical responsibility for pedagogic development. However, feedback requires skill, patience and time, and every *model* retains a right to fallibility. Conversely, a transparent openness about roles, responsibilities and fallibility, at times, might provide an opportunity for MHSWs to restate their professionalism. Finally, data indicates how practical support and assistance for the person's family and social network can support connection and therefore the person's journey to recovery. All of these would require organisational support, and we have noted that a more relational style of management perhaps fits better with the nature of the social work task. Again, balance and equilibrium is vital.

Moreover, organisational support and commitment for more specialised training in personality disorder for MHSWs is seemingly required. MHSWs reported the importance of service users as co-facilitators of education and training more likely to have a direct bearing on practice, given that it has a proven track record in adding value and extending professional understanding, skills, hope and optimism. Some of these features are not necessarily exclusive to social work. However, the profession's ethical obligation to change, empowerment, rights and social justice provides a foundation for a more informed MHSW practice and therefore a more effective contribution to both service users and mental health services. The next chapter will consider these ethical obligations and reassert the value of the relationship in practice; education and training in trauma and the lived experience of personality disorder; support and space for critical thinking about the diagnosis and the person; and finally the importance of collective alliances between service users, practitioners and social work academics to reassert the significance of the social and the relational in policy, procedure and practice.

Summary points

- Balancing the form and content of personality disorder, knowledge of the diagnosis and understanding of the person is crucial to a more informed response to the person.

- Citizenship can be both exclusive and inclusive.

- The person's participation as a co-producer of practice can enhance citizenship.

- A better-informed MHSW practice in the area of personality disorder may be realised through:

  - understanding person and diagnosis;

  - greater transparency and consistency;

  - the provision of feedback;

  - modelling;

  - supporting the person's social and family network;

  - practical support.

Taking it further

Austin, M (2013) *Social Justice and Social Work: Rediscovering a Core Value of the Profession.* Thousand Oaks, CA: Sage.

Dominelli, L and Moosa-Mitha, M (2014) *Reconfiguring Citizenship: Social Exclusion and Diversity with Inclusive Citizenship Practices.* Farnham: Ashgate Publishing.

Gray, M and Webb, S (2013) *The New Politics of Social Work.* London: Palgrave.

Weinstein, J (2009) *Mental Health, Service User Involvement and Recovery.* London: Jessica Kingsley.

6 In pursuit of social justice: what is required?

Critical questions

»   *What are the constituents of a positive conceptualisation of social justice?*

»   *How can therapeutic encounters based on shared understandings promote social justice for people with personality disorder?*

»   *Can prosocial practice inform a human-rights-based approach to working with people with personality disorder?*

»   *What are the conditions for effective, ethical practice in the area of personality disorder?*

Introduction

Our aim, in the preceding chapters, has been to suggest an alternative approach for MHSW understanding and practice in personality disorder, an approach which emphasises balance and equilibrium, recognises interdependence and underlines the value of communication and dialogue. Reflective perhaps of more positive sum approaches to participation and co-production, these features also underline our commonalities as human beings and indeed our shared humanity (Simon, 2007). A drive for equality and parity should be fundamental to our participation as citizens, the distribution of material, political, social and cultural capital and recognition of our strengths and capabilities (Solas, 2008). This drive should not be limited to society per se, but should challenge institutional value patterns (Fraser, 2005), where people are discriminated within '*the very services that are there to, set up to, help protect them*' (Davies et al., 2014).

We saw in Chapter 1 how people with personality disorder can be excluded from general society and mental health services, with the latter in particular reinforcing negative conceptions of self and the escalation of risk (Watts and Morgan, 1994). Moreover, global economic and social inequality is escalating, as is isolation and alienation as a consequence (BASW,

2015a; Lundy, 2011). Having established that people with personality disorder continue to endure isolation and alienation (Tetley et al., 2012), a relationship to social and economic inequality is also apparent. Evidence suggests that higher levels of psychological distress coexist with lower levels of social status (Dalgard, 2008). People with personality disorder can often feel powerless with low levels of self-efficacy skills and social support (Olsson and Dahl, 2012). It is conceivable that support and intervention to empower a person's more constructive response to trauma, connection with self, and sense of belonging might therefore help to counter both psychological and social distress (Dalgard, 2008). MHSW has a role to play. However, we would suggest that MHSW practice should reorientate towards the pursuit of social justice, for maximum effect. Consequently, this chapter will consider the meaning of social justice, suggesting a positive conceptualisation, integrating the distribution of rights with the recognition of strengths and capabilities. The chapter will then consider the essential features of ethical discourse to support the realisation of life as a shared enterprise, dependent on shared understandings for the resolution of social problems. It will then suggest the particular relevance of a human rights approach for practice with people with personality disorder, aligning this specifically with the key features of a relational approach. The chapter will then outline the importance of standards for ethically effective practice, suggesting that when embedded in organisational and practice contexts, these promote the well-being of staff, enhance practice and thereby deliver more effective outcomes for service users. With evidence of the successful implementation of key standards we conclude that there is indeed hope for more effective outcomes for people with personality disorder.

Social justice, distribution and recognition

Social work proclaims an ethical obligation or imperative towards the acquisition of human rights, empowerment and social justice (IFSW, 2014; Reisch and Jani, 2012). There is always the question of how this might be best achieved: through greater opportunity to exercise choice or structural, material and social change. Indeed, we have suggested previously that social work currently is in the eye of a storm between two powerful forces: the rational and technical on the one hand and the situated, responsive and substantive on the other (Kemshall, 2010). Indeed, some have argued that the storm has already passed, as social work appears increasingly aligned with formal technologies of practice (Dustin, 2007). However, if social work is to be an agent of change evidencing respect for human rights and social justice, a rebalancing towards the situated, responsive and substantive is required: a shift more towards empowerment and capacity building to balance the always necessary attention to risk and need (BASW, 2015). The need to understand power relations and the contexts in which discrimination occurs is central to the pursuit of change, rights and justice (ibid.).

The social context, power and powerlessness are critical to the social model, a complementary explanation for the multifactorial nature of health and illness (Duggan, 2002; Plumb, 2005). We saw in Chapter 2 how differences in the acquisition and operation of power impacts on the agency and self-esteem of those less powerful, setting conditions for the establishment of distress patterns: combinations of destructive feelings, thoughts and behaviours (Tew, 2005). While such patterns may encourage the person to believe they can cope with their own, and others' expectations, ultimately these patterns can disconnect the person from self, others and from those close to them. Resonant with evidence of service user research on personality disorder (Castillo, 2003; Castillo et al., 2001; Fallon, 2003; Miller, 1994; Nehls, 1999; Plumb, 2005; Stalker et al., 2005), we would suggest an understanding of power relations, the social context and experience is relevant for understanding personality disorder and the pursuit of social justice for those living with the diagnosis.

Social justice for those experiencing negative power differentials, discrimination and inequality should not just be limited to challenging injustice and inequality, but should advance an enriched conceptualisation of its meaning (Holscher and Bozalek, 2012). Indeed, Fraser (2005) argues that '*social justice requires an enabling – across whatever our differences may be – of everyone's standing as partners in social interaction*' (p 32). Social justice is concerned, on the one hand, with the distribution of rights, resources and opportunities in society (Holscher and Bozalek, 2012). Others argue, however, that justice is a matter of recognising cultural difference (Butler, 1998). Utilitarian and contractual theories of social justice attend, it appears, more to outcome than to process. Clearly, the former defines a just society as one in which institutions are arranged to distribute the greatest happiness for the greatest number (Shackleton, 1972). Nonetheless, happiness is defined independently with no suggestion of how this might be distributed equally within society (Solas, 2008). Contractual theories of social justice emphasise reciprocity for mutual advantage, with justice the result of fairness and agreement (Rawls, 1971). Rawls argued that a '*veil of ignorance*' precluded all knowledge of personal characteristics and social and historical circumstances. People are free and equal, agreeable to the principles of social and political justice (Rawls, 1971). However, Rawls' original position appears somewhat exclusive in that reciprocity is shared only by some, ie those who are free, equal, independent and productive, competent to propose, argue and discuss (Hanisch, 1970). What does this mean for those who, for whatever reason, are not able or thought able to argue the constitution of fairness and political and social justice, in society?

We return to the question of the Other and how we as human beings can split *good* from *bad* in order to defend against that which we perceive or believe to be a threat (Klein, 1959). We have seen, in the preceding chapters, how people with personality disorder can be excluded from mental health services and mainstream society, frequently not seen or heard, with apparent cultural restrictions to their access to resources, rights to treatment and opportunities for hope and recovery, despite legislative change (DoH, 2007; NIMHE, 2003; Wright et al., 2007). If people with personality disorder are to experience greater social justice, an alternative approach to the latter is preferable, one that recognises innate capabilities and the importance of particularity and context, with equal worth (Hanisch, 1970).

Nussbaum (2006) listed ten '*central capabilities*' (p 70) for a life with dignity:

- Life
- Bodily health and integrity
- Senses
- Imagination and thought
- Emotions

- Practical reason

- Affiliation

- Other species

- Play

- Control over our environment.

All of these are vital for social justice, and where one is missing, the latter '*has not been fully done*' (p 77). Attention to capabilities holds the positive value of difference at its core, difference regarded encouragingly and equally rather than as the Other (Klein, 1959). The attainment of well-being is a central, moral concern and that attainment is driven by strengths and capabilities, rather than need and amelioration (Nussbaum and Sen, 1993). Recognition and dialogue is required within an '*inclusive framework*' to '*affirm diversity, difference and the basic human rights of those with whom we disagree*' (Hodge, 2014, p 160). Reflective of our earlier expressed ideas concerning the importance of recognition, balance and dialogue in understanding and working with people with personality disorder, the capability approach stresses the importance of therapeutic encounters based on shared understandings, with practitioners interrogating those structures, ideas and conversations which establish service users as fundamentally different (Wright et al., 2007). Practitioners *and* service users have a right to recognition and to participate equally (Fraser, 2005).

Although some have argued that all human beings are of equal moral concern, it is evident that our labels are '*defined by the more privileged members of society as outside the ambit of moral concern*' (Tronto, 2011, cited in Holscher and Bozalek, 2012, p 1096). It is here then that the pursuits of social justice, those that emphasise distribution and those that emphasise the importance of recognising difference, should converge for the institution of a comprehensive, integrated framework for the advancement of rights and identities that are oppressed and marginalised (Fraser, 1998), a joining of the '*politics of difference and the social politics of equality*' (ibid., p 1). Remembrance of our commonality as human beings should enable respect for difference, including different strengths and capabilities. In many respects the recognition of strengths and capabilities evidences the need for resources and opportunities, both material and structural. Indeed, some have argued that recognition is a predominant feature of social life (Honneth, 1997).

Honneth drew from works positing identity and a stable sense of self grows from relationships which afford mutual recognition (Hegel, 1977; Mead, 1962). Arguing that communication is the primary route towards emancipation, Honneth suggested that self-realisation was dependent on three types of recognition: that which bestows love, care or appreciation; that which confers rights; and finally that which salutes achievements (Honneth, 1997). We would suggest that each form of recognition holds weight for understanding, and working with, a person with personality disorder. We have seen how traumatic social experience, particularly in early life, can impact on personality organisation and identity (Erikson, 1968). Survivors of early life trauma have perhaps not experienced positive object relations with parents or caregivers, where love or care was a mechanism for growing self-confidence (Winnicott, 1957). However, it is possible that care, through empathic recognition and support, can help to repair what was hurt and moreover appreciation of strengths and resilience offers hope for rejuvenation (ibid.; Saleeby, 1997). People with personality disorder have rights to mental health services and treatment; more recent legislative change has assured this (DoH, 2007). However, evidence suggests people can still be excluded, perhaps more because of how person and diagnosis are perceived and labelled, rather than a desert of appropriate treatment (Bateman and Fonagy, 2009; Wright et al., 2007). As a consequence it can be argued, perhaps, that people with personality disorder are not necessarily accustomed to having their strengths acclaimed or accepted.

We have highlighted, in this section, how power, context and experience can both enhance and curtail political and social justice. The relevance of power relations, context and experience for understanding and working with people with personality disorder suggests therefore the significance of the former for challenging injustice *and* for the promotion of social justice for people living with the disorder. The bridging of difference requires recognition and opportunity within a professional relationship which offers protection from *the bond* (Downie, 2011, p 25), driven by care, good communication, empathy and respect to enable trust (Borman, 2011; Stern, 2004). Knowledge of the challenges associated with personality disorder, particularly for practitioners working directly with individuals, leads us to underscore the importance of practitioner resilience, critical engagement and opportunity for support and supervision. Attending to the form and content of distress, the objective and subjective, in equal measure, however, would promote recovery and well-being, while importantly challenging those cultural assumptions which define both person and diagnosis as the Other.

Binary opposites can construct unhelpful identities, limit rights, opportunity and justice (Derrida, 2002). Let us hope that the research findings at the heart of this book go some way to rebalance the more negative representations of personality disorder. When we regard form and content of distress equally, it reflects the policy aspirations for modern, integrated, mental health services, and above all else may enable recognition of strengths as well as needs, opportunity rather than limitation, and hope instead of despair, for the reason that equality enables difference to be respected and to flourish (Malik, 1996). It is evident that social work's ethical principles and codes support social workers to work with strengths for opportunity and hope. Ethical awareness is fundamental to the practice of all social workers (BASW, 2015). The next section will consider certain ethical perspectives which we consider supportive of the intersubjective, contextual and dialogic (Houston, 2009).

Ethical discourse

I recalled in Chapter 4 my personal disappointment, at the very start of my PhD, about the relative lack of social work research and literature in the area of personality disorder. I had expected to find a lot more. Why? Principally because of social work's ethical depth. Members of the UK's national association of social work are bound by its ethical code (BASW, 2012). Moreover, social work has evolved out of humanitarian and egalitarian principles with *'respect for the equality, worth and dignity of all people'* (BASW, 2012, p 16). As an educator I frequently engage students in debates about our *duty* as social workers, the consequences of our intervention and what *makes* social workers 'social workers': social works' deontological, teleological and virtuous commitments (McBeath and Webb, 2002; Reamer, 2005). Given the richness of ethical thought it is perhaps no surprise that I had expected to find a significant amount of social work research and literature about personality disorder. Evidence reveals how the dignity, respect, worth and equality of people with personality disorder can be so easily challenged (Wright et al., 2007). The surprise was, therefore, that I found relatively little.

The complexity of both diagnosis and the experience of personality-related distress lends itself to a plurality of thought. We would suggest that as MHSWs we have a duty to try to understand the experience of living life with a personality disorder, if we are to adhere to our ethical codes (BASW, 2015). Attention to the consequences of our action or non-action is also vital, considering, for example, how being late for an appointment might compound a person's distress and sense of rejection, doubly so if we fail to let them know. Finally, questioning what is personally required for practice in the area of personality disorder is also of relevance. Am I sufficiently wise, perceptive, unprejudiced or audacious? The complexity of practice, in this area as in others, requires a plurality of thought, rooted in a reflexive engagement, funnelled by listening to the Other, speaking only '*as a listener, not an author*' (Young, 1990, p 5). Ethical, moral discourse would appear to support and possibly help realise greater equality and social justice for people with personality disorder (Houston, 2009).

Houston (2009), drawing on the work of Habermas, argues that the recognition of human identity and democratic or egalitarian communication are '*two foundation stones for ethical deliberation in social work*' (p 1274). A moral conversation is that which preserves the liberty and parity of the participants (Habermas, 1990). Any resultant decision is valid if participants and those affected by it agree that as the preferred course of action. However, such agreement is based on accepting the consequences for all. The conversation and decision therefore is riven with a degree of universalisability and an exchange of roles (Houston, 2009). Empathy, the ability to see a situation or position from the other's perspective, is essential to ethical discourse, as is impartiality, '*trying to balance the interests and needs of all the stakeholders*' (ibid., p 1276). We suggested earlier the importance of empathy for practice with personality disorder: understanding trauma as a possible factor in the development of the disorder; balancing attention to form with greater awareness and understanding of the experience of living with the diagnosis; recognising how traumatic experience can limit the survivor's ability to understand the thoughts and reactions of others (Celinski, 2012), all of which may encourage more empathic responses and stronger bonds with the person, for positive and more effective outcomes. We know, for example, that empathy can help to heal what has been hurt, in support of strengths and resilience (Winnicott, 1957).

Ethical discourse which tries to balance the freedom and equality of all parties, with regard to the consequences and which also evidences practitioner empathy for the person, would appear to support a platform for prosocial practice. We saw in Chapter 5 how prosocial practice has been effective in work with people described as hard to engage, or involuntary (Trotter, 2004). Prosocial practice, with its attention to respect, mutuality, transparency, consistency and the deployment of feedback and modelling, offers opportunity to challenge invalidating thoughts and behaviours for the promotion of more prosocial feelings and actions (Cherry, 2005, 2010). Discourse ethics would appear to sustain, therefore, MHSW practice orientated towards the prosocial, in the support of people with personality disorder.

Habermas established certain rules for participation in ethical discourse, in order that power, vested interests and instrumental reason are held in check (Houston, 2009). These rules emphasise the right of the competent speaker to participate, the right to question any assertion, the right to express *'attitudes, desires and needs'* and finally underline how no competent speaker should be prevented from participating and questioning any assertion (ibid.). These guiding rules appear, at first sight, as potentially problematic for practice in the area of personality disorder. We might, for example, question the person's *competence*, their right to question and express any attitude, desire or need. At times we may be right to do so. However, discourse ethics set the preconditions for ethical decision making rather than necessarily guaranteeing an outcome. An ethical decision is that which is fair and unhindered (Houston, 2009). Competing perspectives, thoughts and ideas should be aired constructively, with the aim of reaching at least a compromise, if not agreement. Moreover, dialogue is undoubtedly beneficial *'even when we entertain serious suspicions regarding the rationality of others'* (Weinberg, 2007, p 79).

Social work is committed to equality, human rights, social justice and democracy. Respect for service users is central to these commitments and at the heart of *'ethical and effective practice'* (BASW, 2013, p 8). Ethical discourse, that which is fair and egalitarian, between service user and practitioner, appears vital if social work is to deliver on its commitments and aims. We highlighted in Chapter 5 the importance of understanding both person and diagnosis by all participants of MHSWs. Understanding and demonstrating empathy for the person's position is essential for a fair and equal conversation; it is vital therefore for ethical and effective social work practice (Houston, 2009). Dialogue based on understanding and empathy is one way of bridging our differences (Fraser, 2005). Egalitarian communication (Houston, 2009) appears as an essential feature of a more radically egalitarian social justice, where

> *justice must be done and justice in these circumstances requires equality, so anything that can be done ought to be in order to achieve an equal distribution of benefits, most notably, rights, utilities and capabilities, even when that involves levelling down.*

(Solas, 2008, p 131)

We are suggesting that the depth of social work's ethical thought and commitments establishes a foundation for practice orientated to the prosocial. The emphasis on parity in communication, the recognition of strengths and capabilities within a relationship, where practitioners attend and speak as listeners, underscores the equality and worth of all human beings and offers an appropriate frame for MHSW practice in the area of personality disorder. Discourse ethics, conversations which promote liberty and equality, would support MHSWs' reflexive engagement in their direct work with individuals and in their interrogation of representations of personality disorder. Recognising the person with personality disorder as a human being, not a representative of the Other, is vital, validating experience, its possible constituents, and understanding the implications both for relationships with self, sense of belonging and connections with the wider world. Such an approach to practice would not only challenge the injustice associated with personality disorder, but would importantly promote greater individual and collective justice for people with the disorder while reaffirming social work's founding commitments to humanitarian and egalitarian principles for the attainment of human rights (BASW, 2012).

Human rights and social work

The UK's scaffold for protecting and promoting the human rights of its citizens can appear complex and somewhat fragmented. The United Nations' Universal Declaration of Human Rights (1948) proclaims fundamental human rights to be universally protected for the safeguarding of human dignity (United Nations, 1948). Recognising our inherent dignity, equal and inalienable rights as human beings, it sets the foundation for freedom, justice and peace. Freedom of speech and belief and freedom from fear and poverty are the ultimate aspirations, to be achieved through teaching and education to promote respect for these rights and freedoms in order *'to secure their universal and effective recognition and observance'* (ibid., p 1). Under Article 2, everyone is entitled to these rights and freedoms. Article 7 provides a right to equality before the law and protection from discrimination. Furthermore, Articles 22 and 25 protect social and economic rights to basic needs and services (Healy, 2008).

The European Convention of Human Rights (ECHR) (Council of Europe, 1953), reaffirms our fundamental rights and freedoms in Europe. More recently, the Lisbon Treaty, implemented in 2009 (House of Lords Constitution Committee, 2008), protects human rights, including rights to dignity, equality and justice, under the EU Charter of Fundament Rights (Eur-Lex, 2016). Attempts to distinguish between rights and principles have led some to question member states' interpretation, adherence and implementation of the Charter (Wheeler, 2016). Moreover, its reach, together with the power of the Court of Justice of the European Union (CJEU), has been an extremely sensitive political issue in the UK, given that British courts are able to overturn any British law which breaches the CJEU thereby nullifying Parliament's supreme authority (Boyle, 2016). Nevertheless, three generations of human rights determine our fundamental freedoms and liberty: the first our civil and political rights; the second economic, social and cultural rights such as health; and third our collective rights to peace, a healthy environment and self-determination (Lundy, 2011).

Despite these laudable frameworks and claims about protection, we know that inequality and human rights violations are increasing (ibid.). The economic crash of 2008 has deepened the economic and social inequalities in Europe (Bassell and Akwugo, 2014). In the UK, people with mental health problems are one of the constituency's *'at the sharp end of the assault on public services'*, therefore exacerbating social inequality and worsening mental health problems (Mattheys, 2015, p 475). Demand for mental health services has risen by 20 per cent in the past five years, at the same time as services have had to accommodate an 8 per cent budget cut in real terms (Shah, 2016). Moreover, debt, austerity and unemployment have been linked with an increase in the numbers of British men taking their own lives (Gunnell et al., 2016). The UK's commitment to austerity has clearly not supported its vulnerable citizens' social, cultural and economic rights nor their rights to self-determination. Indeed, the Conservative Party, in their most recent party manifesto, were committed to the repeal of the Human Rights Act (HRA) (1998), a move which some saw as *'legally incoherent'* (European Institute, 2016; Starmer, 2016), given that British courts retain ultimate jurisdiction over the implementation of primary legislation incompatible with the ECHR (Boyle, 2016). However, given that proposals for the repeal of the HRA (1998) had not been published before the UK's decision to leave the European Union (ibid.), it is impossible to foresee how the UK's relationship with the Council of Europe and the ECHR will alter in future years. We can, however, suggest, now with more confidence, that the Charter of Fundamental Rights will almost certainly cease to apply, albeit perhaps with some inevitable 'residual effects' (Barnard, cited in European Institute, 2016, p 7).

It is clear that our human rights framework is complicated and somewhat fragmented, with many questions. The consequences of our most recent decision to leave the European Union will only add to this. However, social work retains and will retain the 'universal and effective recognition and observance[s] of rights' (BASW, 2015a, p 4). A human rights approach to practice necessarily balances equity with equality, is universal in its consideration of life as a shared enterprise, accounts for social and political factors and attends to issues of social justice by recognising the moral imperative of protecting peoples' collective and individual rights (Nelson et al., 2013).

Moreover, social work's history is one of a human rights profession (IFSW, 1988), although it is perhaps important to examine this claim in more detail. Healy (2008) suggests that such a claim has a certain legitimacy given social work's value base, those past activists and previous leaders of the profession and finally social work's historical involvement in human rights struggles. History appears the commonality here. Consequently, some have argued that the profession overstates the case for its incorporation of human rights in theory, policy and practice (Lundy, 2011). Indeed, for some the profession has been complicit in historical injustices (Deepak et al., 2015). It is apparent that the profession's more recent contribution to human rights struggles has been more limited, with correspondingly limited recognition outside of social work itself (ibid.). We would suggest that a prosocial approach to practice in the area of personality disorder would attend to opportunity, distribution, recognising people's strengths and capabilities and consequently promote a rights-based approach to MHSW practice for the betterment of social justice. This book has reminded us of how people with personality disorder are frequently in need of access to treatment and support (DoH, 2007), but can be and still are denied the right to treatment and support, perhaps because of how they are seen by mental health professionals and service providers (NIMHE, 2003; Tetley et al., 2012; Wright et al., 2007).

Practice to promote and protect human rights should empower in order that people know, understand and therefore claim their rights. Moreover, practice and practitioners should hold others to account for the respect, protection and fulfilment of rights (BASW, 2015a). A focus on strengths, participation and capacity should balance the attention to needs and risk (ibid.). This book has aimed to offer an insight into the experience of personality disorder and how this can be reflected in practice contexts. Preceding chapters have suggested the importance of an approach regulated by balance, communication and dialogue, founded on a recognition of our shared humanity. Positive sum methods of engagement will contribute to better outcomes for people with personality disorder because they will begin to challenge the discrimination which surrounds both individuals and diagnosis. Practice to protect and promote people's individual and collective rights would continue to uphold social work's standing as a human rights profession (Healy, 2008; IFSW, 1988). Moreover, realigning the profession to the situated, responsive and substantive would awaken our history of material, structural and social change (Healy, 2008). The professional and practice implications might not just be limited to MHSW practice, but to other areas of social work endeavour as well (HCPC, 2012). We know, for example, that '*a human rights approach involving citizen participation, good leadership and evidence-informed practice can help to reshape economic and social and policies and services*' (BASW, 2015a, p 17). There are clear implications for the profession, practitioners and service users; however, certain conditions for practice will be required.

Conditions for practice

It is evident that if social workers are to uphold effective ethical practice, committed to the protection and promotion of human rights and social justice, a certain environment is required (BASW, 2013). This book has previously suggested that the technical and informational can currently preside over the situational, knowledge and understanding in social work policy and practice. We called in Chapter 3 for greater symmetry between the technical and rational, the situated and substantive. Recognition of ourselves as rational *and* social actors, negotiating our way through the myriad complexity of modern life, underlines the need for compassionate renderings of stereotypical representations so that strengths, as well as risks, can be identified in context and understood in the context of the person's life experience.

Social work, like many other helping professions, is overwhelmed by risk and methods for assessing, calculating and reducing it (Horlick-Jones, 2005). Indeed, some have argued that, given this, '*relational processes remain necessarily subordinate to administrative ones*' (Murphy et al., 2013). Relationship-based practice has been politically contentious for some time, despite support from Munro (Department for Education, 2011) and evidence of the more positive outcomes associated with relationships service users perceive as '*more positive*' (Murphy et al., 2013, p 711). We suggested, in Chapter 3, that any approach to practice should enable social workers to protect and safeguard practices which could present a risk (BASW, 2015a). A relationship founded on respect, dialogue, transparency, consistency and confidentiality will support risk assessment, management and indeed positive risk taking (BASW, 2012; Cherry, 2010). Given this, we cannot support the continual primacy of the administrative over the relational (Murphy et al., 2013), but would argue that the latter should inform the former, in the realisation of more effective outcomes for service users. It is not a matter of reducing social work intervention to a matter of the relationship alone, more that elements of a relational approach are important in every aspect of social work. The research project behind this book suggests that knowledge, understanding, transparency and consistency, the professional use of self, listening and active engagement are crucial features of a relational approach to personality disorder, from which modelling, feedback, social and practical support could be employed to assure more effective outcomes for service users with personality disorder and also MHSWs' contribution to modern, multidisciplinary mental health services. We are perhaps, therefore, suggesting a utilitarian use of the professional relationship appropriate to the context of modern social work practice (Murphy et al., 2013), rather than seeing the relationship as an end in itself. However, clearly, in the current climate even a more utilitarian use of the professional relationship will require certain conditions to be met.

In 2013, BASW set out employers' responsibilities for effective ethical practice, where values and principles of both managers and practitioners are consistent. If we accept NPM is still a significant influence on health and public services, key features of economic and performance efficiency, effective service delivery in the context of reduced resources, service rationing and higher caseloads might not necessarily equate with effective and ethical social work practice (BASW, 2013; Diver, 2008). Similarly, evidence-based practice, as the counterpart to NPM, offers perhaps only a deterministic version of reality, ill-suited to the reflexive engagement and decision making required of social workers (Webb, 2001). Determinism can limit opportunity for partnership, dialogue and negotiation, a reliance on *evidence* can mean, '*by default any room for negotiation, partnership and compromise with the service user is lost*' (Adams et al., 2009, p 300). If social work is obliged to deliver on human rights, empowerment and social justice, as we believe it is, the conditions of NPM and EBP appear unhelpful for effective ethical practice. Indeed, others have argued that a relational style of management is more fitting to the social work task (Ruch, 2012) and, as we have suggested, the promotion and protection of rights and justice. However, it is possible that neither is mutually exclusive as Segal (2012) has argued: relational capacities, such as attunement, self-awareness and sensitivity to relational dynamics, can inform evidence-based interventions, in consultation with the service user.

All employers have a duty to promote the well-being of staff by establishing optimal organisational and environmental conditions, to protect against workplace stress. Management standards cover six primary sources of stress in the workplace. Of particular relevance for social work are those standards which relate to:

- workload demands;

- degree of employee control over workplace arrangements;

- healthy workplace relationships free of unacceptable or discriminatory behaviours;

- the support and information employees receive from colleagues and line managers.
(Health & Safety Executive [HSE], 2010)

The Standards for Employers of Social Workers in England, first launched in 2011, also '*set out shared expectations of employers which will enable social workers in all employment settings to work effectively*' for higher quality service user outcomes (Local Government Association [LGA], 2014). Four of the eight standards relate directly to safe workloads and case allocation; managing risks, including those to personal well-being; access to partnerships to share the best practice and research and supervision, with an emphasis on reflection, learning and development.

Organisational support for and adherence to such standards not only attends to the structural and environmental conditions for effective practice, but also supports individual efforts to protect against work-related stress and increase personal and professional resilience. Evidence suggests that the high levels of stress and burnout associated with social work have contributed to staff shortages, related to both retention and recruitment in many areas of practice (Kinman and Grant, 2011). Coffey et al. (2004) found the highest levels of absenteeism and poorest well-being among social workers employed in children and family settings. Unsurprisingly, job satisfaction was low when compared with other occupational groups (ibid.). Similarly, in MHSW it is evident that the pressures of work and high levels of stress associated with extended working hours cover for vacancies, and the burden of administration can contribute to low levels of job satisfaction, emotional exhaustion and consequent problems in retention and recruitment (Huxley et al., 2005). While structural factors cannot be ignored, evidence suggests that certain individual qualities can predict our resilience to stress: emotional intelligence, aptitude for empathy and reflection and social competence (Kinman and Grant, 2011).

In a study of 240 social work trainees, Kinman and Grant found these qualities key in participants' resilience to stress and consequent emotional and psychological well-being. Interestingly, although emotional and social intelligence evidently protects against stress, both indicate a certain capacity for empathic responses and effective communication with others, including service users. Hence organisational support for the emotional and social intelligence of social work staff may not only contribute to lower levels of stress but also to the enhancement of professional practice (Ruch, 2012). We know that social work staff derive considerable satisfaction from their work (Coffey et al., 2004). Huxley et al. (2005) discovered that participants valued their face-to-face contact with service users very highly, and this indeed was a factor in retention. It is perhaps a question therefore of how employing organisations support staff's capacity for emotional intelligence, empathy, reflection and social competence as a protector against stress, enhanced levels of job satisfaction and for the enhancement of professional practice.

Supportive structures and relationships are believed to be an effective protector against stress (Herman, 1992). We acknowledged earlier the stresses associated with working with someone with personality disorder (Cleary et al., 2002). Clearly, effective supervision and support from team colleagues is vital. Moreover, the absence of effective, reflective supervision would lead to empathic distress, feelings of anxiety and discomfort as a result of witnessing the distress of others (Kinman and Grant, 2011). Empathic distress would undermine rather than enhance the personal well-being of MHSWs and therefore effective practice with people with personality disorder, whereas supervision which attends to the emotional needs of staff can enhance well-being, practice and job satisfaction, by protecting against work-related stress and burnout (Bland and Rossen, 2005). Clearly, adhering to the Standards for Employers (LGA, 2014) would help protect and promote staff well-being, retention and recruitment and enhance the quality of professional practice and the efficacy of service user outcomes in this area of practice, as well as others.

However, it is evident that implementation of the social work standards has been inconsistent across employers, drawing the comment that they are 'one of the best kept secrets in social work' (Schraer, 2015). Furthermore, despite the importance attached to effective, appropriate and reflective supervision in social work (LGA, 2014), recent evidence suggests that supervision remains an elusive entity, limited and variable even for newly qualified social workers (Manthorpe et al., 2015). Despite evidence of the positive impact of supervision on social workers and practice, evidence suggests that opportunity for supervision can be limited by the restrictions on supervisors' time (ibid.). More positively, it is evident that where standards are embedded in organisational structure, culture and day-to-day practice, they herald improvements in the clarity of service structures, safer caseloads, clearer eligibility criteria, effective training and supervision of staff for the engagement and respect of service users and the identification of needs and strengths (Carter, 2015).

It is quite possible that through the setting of conditions for effective, ethical practice (BASW, 2013; LGA, 2014) opportunity for quality partnerships with service users and carers may evolve to offer stronger alliances and additional *evidence* for the resolution of social problems and enhancing the well-being of those subject to discrimination and injustice (Lundy, 2011). After all, experience is a source of knowledge (D'Cruz and Jones, 2004). We have underlined the importance of individual, relational alliances with those who may have experienced early traumatic experience (Knight, 2015). Collective alliances are also important, as a challenge to structural and material forms of discrimination and disadvantage (Blitz et al., 2014). Indeed, some have argued that it is only through service user and practitioner alliance that social work will realise its obligations to those who are marginalised and oppressed (Beresford and Croft, 2004). Cross-discipline and institutional alliances, together with service users, would require agreement on the terms of reference, a commitment to working together for a common goal and ongoing education and support (Blitz et al., 2014). However, social work has the aptitude and capacity to grow these kinds of alliances, as *'forming critical alliances to work collectively for social justice is consistent with social work values and uses social work skills'* (ibid., p 347). Certainly, the challenges surrounding personality disorder, their consequences and the apparent value of a complementary prosocial approach indicates the value of both individual and collective alliances, with social work taking a critical role.

The importance of education and training for MHSWs and other mental health professionals in personality disorder, with particular reference to the value of a prosocial approach, would be essential for building capacity through alliance, especially if such training involved service users as co-facilitators. Founded on the importance of the knowledge, skills and understanding required to form and sustain prosocial relationships (Cherry, 2010), such training would underline the need for respect and empathy for the person, as quite possibly a survivor of early traumatic experience, their rights to treatment and support and recognition as a human being. The involvement of service users as co-facilitators would evidence the importance of socially situated knowledge and many different ways of knowing (Hartman, 1990). The highlighting of the dilemmas associated with access to treatment, support, stigma and discrimination would open a conversation about issues of social justice and injustice, to ignite social workers' critical curiosity (Freire, 1970) and possibly the profession's politics of practice (Reisch and Jani, 2012).

Care would be required to support practical arrangements such as access and payment for co-facilitators in order to avoid the appearance of tokenism (Beresford and Croft, 2001). Perhaps more importantly, the emotional labour of the facilitator with lived experience would need to be recognised and supported (Gregor and Smith, 2009). First, empathy, with *'time to listen and value'* (ibid., p 629) would be required by all, particularly experienced social workers, who may have to witness significant criticism of MHSW practice. Second, there would be a need to absorb the alternative epistemology of the experts by experience, where knowledge is often generated collectively, through conversation, sharing of experiences and networking (Beresford and Branfield, 2006). Knowledge of the complexity of personality disorder and its relationship to trauma would not only need to be co-produced, it would need to be delivered in ways which respect such service user epistemologies. However, the sharing of experiences between experts and MHSWs would generate reflection in and on the moment from which challenges to each defining the other as the Other (Wright et al., 2007) may come. Such training would offer an alternative to those more traditional epistemologies, where the '*professional trainer*' is regarded as the *expert* (Gergen and Gergen, 2003), but it may equip MHSWs to better understand the experience of personality disorder (Marlow and Adamson, 2011).

Setting the conditions for practice which aim to promote safe ways of working, maximise employee control, sustain healthy supportive relationships and partnerships, with opportunity for learning, would protect and promote the well-being of MHSWs, with consequent benefits for retention and recruitment, enhancing practice and service user outcomes. Sustaining professional relationships with people with personality disorder can be both professionally and personally challenging. However, people with personality disorder face immeasurable discrimination, inequality and injustice. We have suggested an approach for MHSW practice based on balance and equilibrium, shared humanity, underlining the value of communication and dialogue. We would argue that such an approach underlines the rights of people with personality disorder for the betterment of social justice. However, such an approach requires certain conditions for practice to assure staff well-being, positive recruitment and retention and most importantly effective outcomes for people with personality disorder.

Conclusion

As much as this chapter has reaffirmed the discrimination surrounding personality disorder, it has also tried to set out an enhanced consideration of social justice, as a matter of distribution, the recognition of strengths and capabilities and conversations across differences. It has suggested the relevance of this conceptualisation for people living with personality disorder. The chapter has stressed the importance of empathic recognition for personal growth, grounded in ethical discourse, with the aim of realising shared understandings about risks and strengths to meet service users' needs. We have outlined social work's historical claims as a human rights profession, while highlighting criticism of the profession's limited incorporation of a human rights approach within contemporary policy and practice. The chapter has suggested how the plight of people with personality disorder is reason for MHSW's reorientation towards a rights-based approach to practice for the betterment of social justice. We would suggest that social work's value base and ethical commitments mean that MHSW is fundamentally equipped to respect equity, equality and therefore protect and promote the collective and individual rights of people with personality disorder. We have suggested, in broad terms, the importance of balancing form with content and the experience of distress, recognising our interdependence and commonality as human beings, underlining the value of communication and dialogue. More specifically, we have suggested the value of experiential knowledge, understanding, transparency and consistency, the professional use of self, listening and active engagement in an approach to people with personality disorder. We would argue that these broad parameters and specific features are suggestive of a prosocial, human rights approach which might advance social justice for people with the diagnosis. It is clear that conditions for practice must be optimised. However, evidence suggests that adherence to the standards for effective ethical practice, learning and development, will support staff, practice and most importantly bring about more effective outcomes for service users. We would conclude therefore that a prosocial approach to personality disorder, facilitated within safe and complementary multidisciplinary mental health services, might offer hope and therefore promote the recovery of people with personality disorder.

Summary points

*   Binary opposites can construct unhelpful identities, limit rights, opportunity and justice.

*   Discourse and dialogue which recognises rights of participation, questioning and expression can support egalitarian social justice.

*   Reflexive engagement, speaking as a listener and recognising the person's human identity, will contribute to the social justice of people with personality disorder.

*   Conditions to enhance practitioners' emotional and social intelligence, reflection and empathy will sustain their resilience and promote more effective outcomes for people with personality disorder.

Taking it further

Abraham, P (2014) *Social Work in Mental Health: Areas of Practice, Challenges, and Way Forward.* Thousand Oaks, CA: Sage.

Austin, M (2013) *Social Justice and Social Work: Rediscovering a Core Value of the Profession.* Thousand Oaks, CA: Sage.

Banks, S (2012) *Ethics and Values in Social Work.* Basingstoke: Palgrave.

Gray, M and Webb, S (2010) *Ethics and Value Perspectives in Social Work.* Basingstoke: Palgrave Macmillan.

Thompson, N (2016) *Anti-discriminatory Practice.* Basingstoke: Palgrave.

Conclusion: a social perspective on personality disorder

Key points

- A more coherent conceptualisation of personality disorder is required.
- Balancing the form of distress with the content of a person's experience can keep the person with personality disorder at the heart of professional practice.
- Traumatic experience should be considered as a possible factor for the development of the disorder.
- A social perspective is founded on humane, empathic, prosocial responses; knowledge of the person and personality disorder; respect, listening to and engaging with the person; broad social supports to promote connection with self, others and the world around
- Social work's history as a human rights profession means MHSW has a contribution to make in the realisation of better outcomes for people with personality disorder.

The premise of this book calls for a more coherent conceptualisation of personality disorder, one to facilitate greater understanding of person and diagnosis so as to promote more effective outcomes for people living with the disorder. Health and illness are known to be multifactorial and dependent on social context, position and the experience of power and powerlessness (Duggan, 2002). Yet the classification of personality disorder appears to take little account of the destructive social experience, namely trauma, as a factor for the development of the disorder in adolescence or early adulthood. Attention is rather focused on the social consequences of the disorder and the functional difficulties the person will experience, particularly in relation to self-direction, empathy and intimacy (APA, 2013). It is of little surprise therefore that some personality disorders are especially associated with separation and divorce (Zimmerman and Coryell, 1989) and severe difficulties in parenting and infant caregiving (Wendland et al., 2014). Moreover, evidence gained from retrospective research studies indicates that neglectful or abusive early relationships are prevalent in the social and relationship histories of people with the diagnosis (Rogosch and Cicchetti, 2005). Intriguingly, Lefebvre et al. (2004) discovered that children with borderline traits were more likely to describe their parents as unaffectionate, aggressive, neglectful, controlling and rejecting. Given such evidence, we have suggested that traumatic experience can be a contributory factor for the development of the disorder. Consequently, trauma should be regarded as a possible explanation for someone's invalidating thoughts, feelings and behaviours, which in turn may encourage a more humane response and therefore more effective outcomes for people with the diagnosis.

Similarities in the experiences of adults with a diagnosis of BPD and children experiencing inadequate parenting have led some to suggest a *'potential prospective pathway from childhood maltreatment to BPD'* (Rogosch and Cicchetti, 2005, p 13). Evidence such as this adds to that from longitudinal research (Massie and Szajnberg, 2008; Sroufe et al., 2005). However, significant doubts remain about whether early childhood trauma contributes to the onset of personality disorder (Paris, 1998). We have argued that the omission of trauma as an aetiological factor leaves us with only a partial conceptualisation of personality disorder, one too reliant on form over and above content (Bracken and Thomas, 2004). Complicated further by questions as to whether personality disorder is separate from or on a continuum with mental illness (Livesley, 2003), we are left with a contested conceptualisation with far-reaching consequences for those so diagnosed and those who love and care for them. Furthermore, the questions surrounding personality disorder – partiality and contest – raise significant implications for mental health professionals, including MHSWs.

We have suggested that too heavy a reliance on form, over and above the experience of living with the diagnosis, can encourage essentialism, the reduction of a person to their essential characteristics, from which responsibility for seemingly negative or dysfunctional behaviours, thoughts and emotions can be attributed (Aviram et al., 2006; Haslam et al. 2006; Goffman, 1990). Essentialism, together with the attribution of responsibility, can induce stigma and stigmatised responses from both the general public and professionally qualified mental health staff, including MHSWs. Indeed, research indicates that mental health professionals are more likely to perceive those who challenge their professional competence and control as *difficult*, rather than ill or deserving help and support (Breeze and Repper, 1998). Challenge and loss can encourage professionals to seek distance from the person, which in turn can contribute to the proliferation of myths and stereotypes about person and diagnosis. Distant, inert relationships can foster alienation and escalate risk to self and others (Watts and Morgan, 1994), whereas knowledge of the person, their history, limitations and strengths can foster greater understanding and empathy for their continuing battle to survive (Nehls, 1998).

We return full circle perhaps to the previously stated need for a more coherent conceptualisation of personality disorder, one which recognises early traumatic experience as a contributory factor. Such a conceptualisation could stimulate the critical curiosity of mental health professionals, including MHSWs, professional understanding and thereby encourage greater empathy for the person in their enduring struggle with life. Relationships centred on understanding, empathy and validation offer antidotes to the person's alienation from self, others and the world around them. They offer hope for a sense of belonging and connection.

We have suggested that social work's alignment with social experience, context, power and position (Parker et al., 1995) establishes a reason for MHSW action in the area of personality disorder. Indeed, our professional standards challenge us to understand the multidimensional nature of human existence, the impact of different experiences, discrimination and strengths (HCPC, 2012). Moreover, the complexity of the disorder indicates the importance of identifying reasons for thoughts, feelings and behaviours. Without reason and explanation the risk of alienation and estrangement is sustained. Understanding, empathy and hope can promote recovery and more effective outcomes for people with the diagnosis. We have suggested that for these reasons, MHSW has a role to play in emphasising the relevance of a social perspective on personality disorder, in part to hold the foci of professionals on both the form the diagnosis assumes *and* on the experience of living with it. This book has outlined the key features of a social perspective on personality disorder:

- To recognise and understand the impact of early traumatic experience.

- To value humane, empathic prosocial responses.

- To give importance to the knowledge of the person and personality disorder.

- To respect, listen to and engage with the person.

- To know the value of broad social supports to promote connection with self, others and the world around them.

Its value lies in its potential for understanding contributory factors, consequences and crucially for its reaffirmation of the professional relationship as a mechanism for positive change. Empathic relationships which offer the *'protection of the bond'* (Downie, 2011, p 25) and evidence, mutual respect, reliability and confidentiality may enable opportunity, the identification of personal strengths and the value of broad social supports. It is the restoration of our connection with self and others that lies at the heart of hope for people with personality disorder. Effective prosocial relationships support people's understanding of self and moreover offer opportunity to test alternative, more adaptive ways of relating. When coupled with broad social supports, a greater sense of belonging and connection may ensue which, as we know, are vital to the restoration of self after acute or sustained trauma (Herman, 1992). Believing in the possibility of change is vital.

Social work's theoretical heritage centres on the subject, seeing those with vulnerabilities and presenting problems as inherently social selves (Philip, 1979). Moreover, our current knowledge and standards for practice underline the importance of relational skills, understanding and partnership to promote well-being and respond to threats, including those which result from discrimination, disadvantage and oppression (HCPC, 2012). We would suggest therefore that the history of social work together with its current standards (HCPC, 2012) offer MHSW a paradigm for practice in this area. Through affirming the importance of understanding, empathic prosocial relationships and broad social supports, MHSW would not only underline its contribution to modern mental health services but would also offer hope for more effective outcomes for people with personality disorder.

Chapter 1 introduced our critical consideration of the diagnosis and what we perceive to be the key fault lines at its heart: questions about its nature; competing explanations; the primacy of form over content and questions about the efficacy of treatment, especially psychotropic medication. Our brief review of the seminal literature on personality disorder reveals the depth of controversy and ambiguity associated with those past revisions which attempted to assert its distinct nature (Cleckley, 1982; Pinel, 1801; Prichard, 1837) or evidence of its continuity with normal personality or other mental disorders (Jaspers, 1963; Schneider, 1958). We highlighted the questions surrounding BPD specifically. We then moved to review and critique the differences with the more recent classifications (APA, 1994; WHO, 1992), paying particular attention to the most recent revision, DSM V (APA, 2013), originally conceived as a means of bridging categorical *and* dimensional approaches. However, we note that following significant criticism, a more categorical approach has been retained.

The chapter moved on to consider the key perspectives, psychiatric, psychological and social, including service users, which offer a wealth of knowledge and explanation of personality disorder. However, it is clear from a review of the psychological perspective, which views personality disorder as a maladaptive variant of normal personality disorder (Ro et al., 2012), that key explanations can compete rather than complement one another. We evidently have the tools to work more effectively with personality disorder. It is a question of whether we are using these tools in the most effective way. If we accept that form can predominate over content (Bracken and Thomas, 2004), there is much to be gained from attending to power differentials and the process by which negative attributes of difference can be internalised. A social perspective may concentrate our focus on the reasons for someone's thoughts, feelings and behaviours, indeed the reasons behind their personal distress patterns (Tew, 2005). Attending to and maintaining a focus on the social may not only help us to balance the form of personality disorder with its experience, but also help us to utilise our explanatory frameworks in more complementary ways. The social perspective would help mental health professionals maintain a focus on the person's experience and actual identity, rather than on what is assumed (Goffman, 1990). It might therefore promote understanding while challenging the stigma and discrimination which continues to surround the diagnosis (NIMHE, 2003; Tetley et al., 2012).

Evidence proves that people with personality disorder are frequently perceived as difficult, especially when believed to be challenging professional competence and control (Breeze and Repper, 1998). This triggers a cycle of malignant alienation and the progressive deterioration of the professional relationship through a loss of sympathy and support (Watts and Morgan, 1994). We suggested in Chapter 1 that such a process undermines knowledge and understanding, as well as the effective recognition of distress, risk assessment and management. We have argued that recognising early traumatic experience as a contributory factor for the development of personality disorder would stimulate professional curiosity, understanding and empathy for the person's experience, its consequences and their ongoing struggle with life. We know that acute and/or chronic trauma can disconnect the person from self, others and the world around them, whereas knowledge, understanding and empathy can only enhance connection and a sense of belonging. Risk assessment and risk management might be reliably enhanced and outcomes more reliably effective. A social perspective on personality disorder can hold the focus of attention on the person's experience and crucially their experience of distress. Such a focus can challenge the assumptions surrounding the diagnosis and promote understanding, empathy and more effective outcomes.

The recognition of trauma as an aetiological factor for the development of personality disorder appears critical to this path.

We considered the relevance of trauma for understanding and working with personality disorder in more detail in Chapter 2. We cited evidence to argue that trauma features in the experience of many people living with mental disorder, including personality disorder (Read et al., 2004). Given that trauma impacts on personality organisation and identity (Erikson, 1968), we suggested its relevance as an explanatory frame. There is a continuing need therefore for mental health professionals to be trauma informed. Recognising the impact of acute or chronic trauma, especially in early years, could encourage more empathic practice to undercut stigma and exclusion and promote more effective outcomes and recovery. We argued that social work's requirement to understand how diverse constituents shape human existence (TCSW, 2012) places an onus on MHSW to articulate the relevance of trauma for understanding, empathy and outcomes.

The chapter recognised the universality of risk alongside the uniqueness of the person's experience and response to it. In a more detailed consideration of the DSM V (APA, 2013) definition, we distinguished between acute traumatic accidents, damaging events and relationships repeated over time (Lee, 2006). Vulnerability to both forms is particularly heightened in childhood. Early traumatic experience can impact on social functioning, defence mechanisms, cognition, memory processing and also increase the risk of psychiatric disorder in adulthood (Massie and Szajnberg, 2008; Sroufe et al., 2005). Indeed, trauma can significantly affect adult personality, ego strength and the person's ability to master threats (Erikson, 1968). Struggling to cope with the developing self, relationships can become compromised or otherwise impaired over time and across situations (APA, 2013). Moreover, the trauma survivor faces a higher risk for re-traumatisation (Briere and Hodges, 2010). Despite the pervasiveness of risk and its significant implications, evidence suggests that trauma can frequently be overlooked as a personal trouble and public issue (Mills, 1970). We argued that this may relate to the predominance of PTSD which clouds the uniqueness of trauma for each individual (Kirmayer et al., 2007). It is also possible that the risks associated with working with trauma survivors (Figley, 1995; Herman, 1992; McCann and Pearlman, 1990; Munroe et al., 1995) lead us, as mental health professionals, to employ avoidance strategies to gain distance and protect our own mental, emotional and physical well-being (Watts and Morgan, 1994). However, evidence suggests that satisfaction, social support and reflection are factors which enhance the resilience of mental health professionals working with trauma survivors (King et al., 1998; Stamm, 1999; Wilson et al., 2011). Effective supervision will ensure that mental health professionals can sustain an awareness of trauma, its uniqueness and relevance for understanding personality disorder.

We considered the association between trauma and personality disorder in some detail, suggesting an association with the development of symptoms and the diagnosis itself. The association is significant not only in numerical terms (Bandelow et al., 2005; Zanarini, 2000) but also in relation to co-morbidity. Childhood maltreatment, the experience of injury and life-threatening events have been associated with schizotypal symptoms, particularly in men (Berenbaum et al., 2008). Moreover, the severity of abuse has been associated with the severity of symptoms (Zanarini et al., 2002). Indifferent, chaotic or pensive attachments are associated with certain forms of personality disorder, ie schizoid and anti-social personality disorder (Head et al., 1991; Patterson et al., 1989). Evidence, including that from longitudinal research (Massie and Szajnberg, 2008; Sroufe et al., 2005), warrants the attention of mental health professionals to further inform our therapeutic interventions.

Personality disorder has genetic, social and psychological determinants (Laulik et al., 2013). The association with trauma alone, a complex if not uniquely personal experience, suggests that no one discourse holds a primacy of explanation. Indeed, trauma's temporal and multidimensional nature demands it is understood in the political, social, cultural and personal context in which it occurs. We conclude in Chapter 2 that a more coherent conceptualisation of personality disorder is required, within which each professional discourse plays a part. Moreover, a more balanced understanding and response to the person with personality disorder would manage risk more effectively and encourage strength and resilience. However, the recognition of trauma raises implications for the practice of mental health professionals given that a more empathic, compassionate approach to the person with personality disorder is required (NIMHE, 2003). We know that empathy can inhibit anti-social behaviours (Eisenberg et al., 2005), promote healthy personal development (Hoffman, 2001), minimise aggression towards others (Weisner and Silbereisen, 2003) and therefore lead to more effective outcomes (Forrester et al., 2008). We have argued that the person with personality disorder should indeed be at the centre of all our endeavours, grounding our understanding of and response to the diagnosis. Human experience is after all our source of commonality as people and mental health professionals. There is a need for our different professional lenses to reflect both inwards and outwards, in order that we recognise and accept disciplinary differences and commonalities in the best interests of people with personality disorder.

We have suggested that each discourse has an equal part to play; the psychiatric informs our understanding of form and response to treatment; the psychological offers a broader appreciation of subjective reality; the expert by experience details the uniqueness of personal experience in its particular social, cultural and political context; the social emphasises the importance of experience as a contributor to and consequence of mental distress. Moreover, a social perspective underlines the value of broad social supports and the importance of the professional relationship as a mechanism for positive change (Cherry, 2005). Indeed, the HCPC (2012) expects social workers to understand the multidimensional nature of human existence and the impact of social structures on individuals, groups and communities. We have argued that the value of the social perspective and the expectations which surround it (BASW, 2015b; HCPC, 2012) give voice to the need for MHSW action in the area of personality disorder. However, this has implications for the profession at a time of increasingly technical and administrative processes in practice (Dustin, 2007).

MHSW has a contribution to make to enhance the understanding of, and empathy for, people with personality disorder. Traditionally social work has occupied a liminal space between binary opposites, between the private and the public, the subject and the object, between the rational/technical, the socially situated and the responsive (Kemshall, 2010). We analysed the implications of these drivers in Chapter 3, in the context of society's ever-increasing need to assess, predict and manage risk (Beck, 1992). We argued that risk is an embedded social activity and therefore impossible to eliminate even with the aid of technical and rational methods. The chapter considered the development of the technical and rational in *progressive* society and suggested the predominance of these facets over the substantive, social and the relational (Weber, 2012). Risking disconnection from our creative will and our right to act as socially confident actors, we argued the predominance of the rational and technical can alienate those vulnerable and less advantaged at '*fateful moments*' (Giddens, 2013). The chapter suggested the need to recognise the mutual importance of the technical and the substantive, our rational *and* our social selves. While technical methods may help us to identify risk, it is our social selves that enable us to negotiate it.

We moved on in Chapter 3 to offer a critique of recent social policy suggesting a popular reliance on '*rational actors*' and more technical means for investigating and redressing the *problem* of risk. We argued that a relationship between mental disorder, risk and violence should not simply be assumed (Corbett and Westwood, 2005). However, policy has clearly prioritised public safety, control and service rationing over and above reasons for distress and the likely relationship to social situations. The chapter reviewed policy specific to personality disorder (NIMHE, 2003) and suggested that an absence in recent years underlines the need to close the equality gap if we are to improve access to therapeutic services for people with the diagnosis (DoH, 2009, 2010). We argued legitimate policy objectives need to be realised through relationships which demonstrate empathy for the person's social experience, knowledge and understanding of the reasons for their distress. As we are both rational and social actors, a sole reliance on the technical in policy and practice is insufficient. Our rational and social selves need to be understood as interdependent and in balance. If interventions are to span both the technical and relational, a technology of the relationship is required (Parton, 2008).

The importance of the social and the relational is considered in the context of practice heavily influenced by the technical, rational, risk and a preoccupation with the market (Webb, 2006). We considered social work's liminal status in the later sections of Chapter 3 in more detail: its principal foundations in human rights, collective responsibility and respect for diversity alongside its duty to safeguard against risk and harm, while upholding personal autonomy. Here lies the essence of social work's social and rational boundaries and the essence of social workers' identities as both social and rational actors (Kemshall, 2010). We are required to straddle both worlds. However, too close a proximity to either is unhelpful for practitioners and ultimately for the people they work with. Although we accept social work's role in governmentality (Foucault, 1997) and the need for objective knowledge, we argue that we are now over-reliant on the technical and rational in practice. A realignment to the subject, social and relational, is required, as after all the primary task of social work places the person at the centre: it is our relationships with them which matter the most (Ruch, 2012; Wilson et al., 2011).

If social work is to ever deliver on its commitment to the subject and their voice, the interpersonal and analytical skills of social workers will be evermore essential. Interpretation of context, language and meaning is and will be vital, together with the continued professional use of self and the ability to hold competing perspectives in balance. Not only would this evidence respect for the person and generate knowledge to inform positive risk taking in general (McBeath and Webb, 2002), the proposition has particular relevance with the plight of people with personality disorder. We know that people with personality disorder can be excluded from mental health services (NIMHE, 2003; Wright et al., 2007), practice evidencing respect, interpersonal and analytical skills, and the professional use of self may enable service user inclusion to generate knowledge of the subject to inform risk assessment, management and most importantly help deliver life-long learning and more effective outcomes (Tew et al., 2012). However, it is evident that such an approach would require opportunities for practitioner reflection, reflexivity and effective supervision within a fitting organisational context (Ruch, 2012).

We argued that social work's organisational context, in the UK at least, has become increasingly orientated to the demands of NPM: performance management and regulation through inspection and audit (Clarke and Newman, 1993). Although such managerial approaches may serve to bolster our fragile confidence in organisational and social structures, they seem somewhat incompatible with an endeavour which holds the unpredictability of human behaviour close to its heart. Risk and need are perhaps not best served by an approach which prioritises measurement and efficiency above all else (Dustin, 2007). Separation from or denial of the unpredictable nature of humankind can induce an anxious, avoidant or defensive management stance. This is interestingly reflective of an approach taken with personality disorder (Aviram et al., 2006). We know the latter can induce a desire for distance from the person, which can compound the latter's sense of alienation, and susceptibility to risk (Watts and Morgan, 1994). Unsurprisingly we suggested that social work's management structures should more helpfully reflect the nature of the profession's primary task and the central place of human beings within this (Ruch, 2012). We have argued for the importance of shared understandings about practice (Norton, 2012, Chapter 15) and the value of reflection, reflexivity and principles of relational management to support the promotion of a relationship-based approach to practice. Although this may appear contradictory, given the challenges associated with personality disorder, we argue that a relationship-based approach focusing on what is at stake for the persons is relevant for practice in this area (Kleinman, 1999). Considering the importance of the relational for practice and management leads us to the heart of this book, the chapters which report on the project's empirical findings and therefore convey some of what is at stake for service users with personality disorder and MHSWs.

Chapter 4 began by acknowledging the key pointers for change within recent policy and legislation (DoH, 2014): the importance of supporting well-being through integrated working; working to peoples' strengths; supported self-assessment; independent advocacy and the importance of voice and rights (DoH, 2015a). We suggest that emphases such as these contextualise a different approach to working with personality disorder, which this book with the research findings at its heart may contribute to. A summary of personal professional experience informed, as it was, by service user narratives of exclusion and overwhelming personal distress, sets the context and details our personal disappointment at the apparent lack of social work research relevant to personality disorder, highlighting this as a key driver for initiating a research project which took seven years to complete.

The research questions focused on how service users understand and experience personality disorder and MHSW practice. These required a design and methodology to explain the relative nature of experience and moreover appreciate experience as a source of knowledge. As Chapter 4 gathered pace, we reflected on the value of postmodern, constructivist and critical ideas for grappling with the complexity of the disorder and the relative nature of experience. We also reflected on the value of adopting a reflexive approach to appreciate participants' understandings of their position in multiple worlds. Reflection and reflexivity enabled us to negotiate our own interpretative frame as a former MHSW experienced in working with people with personality disorder. The apparent lack of MHSW research about personality disorder (Keys and Lambert, 2003) underlined the need for this project to generate a product, a grounded theory relevant to both personality disorder and MHSW. The adoption of CGT (Charmaz, 2008) meant that the research product, the grounded theory, was both relevant and prioritised the studied world (ibid.). We revealed how this grounded theory illuminates ways in which the disorder is understood and experienced, underlining the value of humane, empathic and prosocial relationships. The latter are in part dependent on the professional use of self to generate the person's active engagement and interest. The theory suggests that stronger professional bonds, supported by broad social supports, may promote a greater sense of connection with self and others and therefore empower a more positive response to trauma and ultimately more effective outcomes.

The data included in Chapter 4, from interviews with both service users and MHSWs, reveals how personality disorder is a complex, multifaceted disorder, which resists singular explanation. It is apparent that the uncertainty, contest and complexity which surrounds it can impair understanding and consequently fuel negative and distant responses from the general public and mental health professionals alike. Rejection, resignation, fear and denial can characterise the response to the person and contribute to the stigma and discrimination which can separate the person from the mainstream. Professional distance can then be legitimised, which serves to reinforce the person's distress, sense of difference and exclusion, with the result that both service users and MHSWs can come to construct the other, as the Other (Wright et al., 2007). Data from both samples serves to explain personality disorder in relation to traumatic experience with service users and MHSWs describing the experience of distress as centred on loss, isolation, overwhelming emotions, intense reactions, patterns of behaviour and projections. The distress associated with personality disorder can be complex, frightening and overwhelming. And yet the person can still be excluded from sources of help, treatment and recovery (Tetley et al., 2012). We suggested the expression of distress can be both a demonstration of survival and a cry for help (Tew, 2002), which underlines in turn the importance of dialogue, reciprocity and the importance of the MHSW as an enlightened witness (ibid.).

Chapter 4 underlined the importance of practice which attends to interpretation, meaning and the interpersonal to nourish more caring bonds to help ensure better outcomes for people with a personality disorder. Data from Phases 1 and 2 emphasised the importance of the MHSW gaining knowledge of both the person and diagnosis through a professional sense of self, respect, listening and active engagement. Indeed, we suggested knowledge of the diagnosis can be a protective factor for the MHSW, helping to sustain their involvement in the face of significant interpersonal challenges. While we acknowledged the challenges frequently associated with personality disorder and survivors of trauma, we argued that the experience of chronic or acute trauma demands a humane response to help ensure better access to treatment, support and therefore more effective outcomes. We know that connection and a sense of belonging can be the most effective antidote to traumatic experience (Herman, 1992). We suggested that broad social supports are perhaps as important for generating a sense of connection and belonging. The value of practical support, encouragement and working alongside the person, facilitating the involvement of others and/or supporting the person's social and family network should not be underestimated. Evidence suggests that service users value broad social supports over and above more specialist, professional interventions (Ikkos et al., 2011). Having established the fundamentally important elements of practice – knowledge, understanding, empathy and broad social supports – we moved on in Chapter 5 to consider how MHSW practice with people with a personality disorder might be better informed.

Our assertion that MHSW has a part to play in advancing a more coherent and balanced conceptualisation of personality disorder was considered in more detail in Chapter 5, particularly in relation to how MHSW practice may be better informed. We suggested enhancements in understanding and practice are dependent upon recognising service users as citizens with both rights and obligations. Indeed, we support the more active conceptualisation of citizenship which respects rights, obligations, freedoms and contributions (Lister, 2007). We considered citizenship as it relates to this project emerging from a policy context which has stressed the importance of service user and public involvement in the design, delivery and implementation of services (Alford, 1998). The chapter considered the meaning of co-production, while firmly asserting the value of positive sum approaches, those which emphasise complementary roles, negotiation and dialogue. While not making any claims of co-production, we suggested that the project respects all participants as citizens especially given the importance it attaches to interdependence, interaction and dialogue. In this sense Chapter 5 builds on those findings from Chapter 4 which highlighted a commonality of thought about personality disorder, ie the relevance of trauma; intensity of distress; the value of the relational and broad social supports. From commonalities such as these we may begin to bridge our differences, our different understandings and experiences of personality disorder, for better-informed practice.

Chapter 5 revealed the importance of understanding both person *and* diagnosis; indeed, there is considerable commonality across service users and MHSWs about the importance of understanding the person, the diversity of need and experience in order to avoid the attribution of stereotypical assumptions. The value of dialogue for understanding the diversity of experience and self is immeasurable, as it is for supporting greater transparency and consistency for better-informed practice. The data in Chapter 5 highlights factors which can so easily compromise transparent and consistent practice, especially high turnover in staff, contexts and technologies of practice. However, data suggests that dialogue can help reformulate that which we perceive to be a problem (Livesley, 2003) to secure transparency and consistency from which people can learn more stable ways of relating to self and others. While greater transparency and consistency may offer a context, it is insufficient as a source of learning in itself. Data in Chapter 5 clearly identified feedback, both individual and collective, as a source of learning, a means by which people can *self-develop*. People who have experienced trauma in their earlier lives may never have had an opportunity to learn from the feedback offered by a caregiver or parent. Moreover, feedback can be an important source of motivation, evidencing social support. While service users and MHSWs concurred on the value of feedback as a source of validation, MHSW participants highlighted key differences: how the context and complexity of social work can mitigate opportunities for feedback, particularly in light of possible deficiencies in time, patience and skill. The value of investment in training, education and relational management are highlighted.

Clark (2006) argues that social work has a pedagogical role. The data included in Chapter 5 points to this history, in that service users and MHSWs suggest the value of modelling and the ability to inspire just by being, '*living a "normal life" in the real world*'. While the data reminds us that MHSWs are not unique and moreover can be fallible, themes within it suggested the relevance of prosocial practice, that which asserts the value of transparency, consistency, feedback and modelling to validate the person and, moreover, to challenge invalidating thoughts, feelings and behaviours (Cherry, 2005, 2010; Trotter, 2004). We noted the efficacy of prosocial approaches with those subject to statutory intervention or described as '*hard to engage*' (ibid.). Chapter 5 also revealed some commonality about the value of supporting the person's family and social network. However, MHSWs again pointed to the ways in which different contexts, complexities and deficiencies in resourcing can mitigate. The data reaffirmed the importance of MHSWs' genuine interest and curiosity, rather than distance and avoidance, to empower a more constructive response to traumatic experience. Establishing or maintaining individual connections can help repair what was hurt (Winnicott, 1973). The data suggested the value of broad social and practical supports to complement the individual and, moreover, to promote the co-operative use of power and shared under-standings for greater collaboration between service user and MHSW.

We cited earlier the central importance of investment in training and education for better-informed practice with people with personality disorder. Data in Chapter 5 revealed how some MHSWs are quite clear about the value of experts by experience as co-facilitators of education and specialised training in the diagnosis. Expert facilitators, drawing on their personal experience, add value, efficacy and moreover would emphasise our commonalities as human beings and the humanity we share as service users, MHSWs and mental health professionals. Through challenging traditionally stigmatising assumptions, co-facilitated training could increase professional optimism to complement the emergent therapeutic opti-mism about the treatment of personality disorder (Bateman and Fonagy, 2000; Lamont and Brunero, 2009).

Chapter 5 left us with some key commonalities across both service users and MHSWs:

*   The relevance of trauma for understanding the diagnosis and experience of personality disorder.
*   The intensity of personality-related distress.
*   The value of the relational and broad social supports.

Consensus on the key factors to better inform practice are also evident:

*   Understanding the person and the diversity of their experience and needs.
*   The importance of transparency and consistency, feedback and modelling.
*   Supporting the person's social and family network.
*   The value of broad, social and practical support.

Differences between service users and MHSWs centre on the diverse complexities and contexts of practice together with the fallibility of MHSWs and perhaps social work organisations. Co-facilitated, specialised training in personality disorder may offer opportunities for greater dialogue between service users and practitioners from which differences can be explored and commonalities further developed. Understandings to challenge each other as the Other (Klein, 1959) may then emerge for the promotion of social justice.

Chapter 6 considered the meaning of social justice and social work endeavours on behalf of vulnerable people (IFSW, 2014). Again we suggested the importance of a positive sum approach which emphasises the distribution of rights *and* the recognition of strengths and capabilities. Indeed, we argue that the pursuit of social justice involves more than a challenge to inequality, through the incorporation of shared interactions to bridge difference (Fraser, 2005). The chapter reviewed utilitarian and contractual approaches to social justice, arguing that reciprocity is not just for the *rational* but for all, in that everyone's capabilities should be recognised and valued with equal worth (Hanisch, 1970). Drawing on the work of Nussbaum (2006) we suggested the value of the capability approach, with its emphasis on particularity, context and the positive value of difference, for understanding and working with personality disorder. It supports the need for therapeutic encounters based on shared understandings to challenge stereotypical assumptions and evidence care, recognise people's rights and achievements (Honneth, 1997). We argued that the richness and plurality of social work's ethical thought, with its deontological, teleological and virtuous commitments (McBeath and Webb, 2002), supports a more reflexive practice with people with personality disorder (Young, 1990). Recognition of human identity, supported through egalitarian or democratic communication to demonstrate empathy and a concern for the interests of all (Houston, 2009), offers a foundation for a more prosocial approach to working with personality disorder (Cherry, 2005, 2010). It sets the context for the recognition of strengths, capabilities and shared understandings to underscore the equal worth of human beings and their entitlement to civil, political, economic, social and cultural rights.

Chapter 6 considered social work's somewhat contested history as a '*human rights profession*' alongside the rather complicated and fragmented legal and organisational framework for the advancement of human rights. We suggested the value of a human rights approach to practice, one which balances equity with equality, recognises life as a shared enterprise and most importantly recognises a moral imperative to protect and advance people's collective and individual rights. Such an approach would advance the rights of people with personality disorder while also going some way to reclaim contemporary social work's history as a human rights profession. However, we argued that a certain organisational environment is required, one which reflects an understanding of the rational and social elements of human nature and therefore social work practice. While not reducing practice to the relational alone, we argue that the relational should inform every aspect of practice and that the latter should not be dependent on the technical and rational alone (Murphy et al., 2013). Effective, ethical practice is dependent on the correct environmental and organisational conditions (HSE, 2010). Chapter 6 called for the consistent implementation of employers' standards (GLA, 2014), including those which frame effective supervision and support, to help ensure the retention and recruitment of professional, qualified social work staff. Strategies to enhance individual, collective and structural relationships will embolden the emotional and social intelligence of staff for greater personal and professional resilience, aptitude for empathy, critical curiosity and therefore the politics of our profession.

This work represents the culmination of a project which spans at least 12 years. It has evolved out of a commitment to work for positive change and a belief in social work's capacity to enact this, in collaboration with others. These commitments and beliefs have sustained this project and have consequently grounded this work, a work which calls for a more coherent conceptualisation of the diagnosis, one which recognises traumatic experience as an aetiological factor relevant for understanding the experience of personality disorder, an enhanced focus on experience and what is at stake for the person to encourage professional curiosity, understanding, empathy and validation, all of which are vital in the challenge to stigma, inequality and discrimination. Holding our focus on the person would enable us to utilise our disciplinary perspectives in more effective, complementary ways. After all an interest in the complexity of human experience is what is common to all social work and health professionals. Social work's theoretical heritage and standards of practice suggests that the profession has a particular role to play in affirming the value of empathic prosocial relationships and broad social supports for people with personality disorder. MHSW would not only therefore underline its contribution to modern mental health services but enhance its contribution to inspiring hope for the many people living life with a diagnosis of personality disorder.

References

Adams, R, Dominelli, L and Payne, M (2009) *Practising Social Work in a Complex World*. London: Palgrave Macmillan.

Alderman, S (2008) From Trauma to Resilience. In Parens, H, Blumm H, and Akhtar, S (eds), *The Unbroken Soul: Tragedy, Trauma and Resilience*. Maryland, USA; Jason Aronson (Chapter 9).

Alexander, M and Mohanty, C (1997) *Feminist Genealogies, Colonial Legacies, Democratic Futures*. New York: Routledge.

Alford, J (1998) A Public Management Road Less Travelled: Clients as Co-producers of Public Services. *Australian Journal of Public Administration*, 57(4): 128–37.

Allport, G W (1938) *Personality: A Psychological Interpretation*. New York: Holt.

American Psychiatric Association (APA) (1980) *Diagnostic and Statistical Manual of Mental Disorders* (3rd edn). Washington DC: APA.

American Psychiatric Association (APA) (1994) *Diagnostic and Statistical Manual of Mental Disorders* (4th ed). Washington, DC: American Psychiatric Association.

American Psychiatric Association (APA) (2012) Diagnostic and Statistical Manual of Mental Disorders (5th ed). *American Psychiatric Association*. [online] Available at: www.dsm5.org/Documents/Personality%20Disorders/DSM-IV%20 and%20DSM-5%20Criteria%20for%20the%20Personality%20Disorders%205-1-12.pdf (accessed 11 February 2013).

American Psychiatric Association (APA) (2013) Post-traumatic Stress Disorder. [online] Available at: www.dsm5.org/Documents/PTSD%20Fact%20Sheet.pdf (accessed 31 July 2014).

Angermeyer, M C and Matschinger, H (2003) The Stigma of Mental Illness: Effects of Labelling on Public Attitudes towards People with Mental Disorder. *Acta Psychiatrica Scandinavia*,108(4): 304–9.

Arnstein, S (1969) Ladder of Citizen Participation. *Journal of the American Institute of Planners*, 35(4): 216–24.

Ashton, M C and Lee, K (2001) A Theoretical Basis for the Major Dimensions of Personality. *European Journal of Personality*, 15: 327–53.

Atkinson, P and Coffey, A (1997) Analysing Documentary Realities, in Silverman, D (ed) *Qualitative Research: Theory, Method and Practice* (pp 45–62). Thousand Oaks, CA: Sage.

Aviram, R, Brodsky, B and Stanley, B (2006) Borderline Personality Disorder, Stigma and Treatment Implications: Prevalence and Correlates of Personality Disorder. *British Journal of Psychiatry*, 14(5): 249–56.

Baehr, W (2001) The 'Iron Cage' and the 'Shell as Hard as Steel': Parsons, Weber, and the Stahlhartes Gehäuse Metaphor in the Protestant Ethic and the Spirit of Capitalism. *History & Theory*, 40(2): 153–69.

Bailey, D and Liyanage, L (2012) The Role of the Mental Health Social Worker: Political Pawns in the Reconfiguration of Adult Health and Social Care. *The British Journal of Social Work*, 42(6): 1113–31.

Balen, R, Rhodes, C and Ward, L (2010) The Power of Stories: Using Narrative for Interdisciplinary Learning in Health and Social Care. *Social Work Education*, 29(4): 416–26.

Ball, J S and Links, P S (2009) Borderline Personality Disorder: Evidence for a Causal Relationship. *Current Psychiatric Reports*, 11(1): 63–8.

Bandelow, B, Krause, J, Wedekind, D, Broocks, A, Halek, G and Ruther, E (2005) Early Traumatic Life Events, Parental Attitudes, Family History, and Birth Risk Factors in Patients with Borderline Personality Disorder and Healthy Controls. *Psychiatry Research*, 134(2), 169–79.

Barnes, M, Harrison, S, Mort, M and Shardlow, P (1999) *Unequal Partners: User Groups and Community Care*. Bristol: Policy Press.

Bassel, L and Akwugo, E (2014) Solidarity under Austerity: Intersectionality in France and the United Kingdom. *Politics & Gender*, 10(1): 130–6.

Bateman, A and Fonagy, P (2001) Treatment of Borderline Personality Disorder with Pyschoanalytically Oriented Partial Hospitalisation: An 18 month follow up. *American Journal of Psychiatry*, 158(1): 36–42.

Bateman, A and Fonagy, P (2004) *Psychotherapy for Borderline Personality Disorder: Mentalization-Based Treatment.* Oxford: Oxford University Press.

Bateman, A and Fonagy, P (2006) *Mentalization-Based Treatment for Borderline Personality Disorder: A Practical Guide.* Oxford: Oxford University Press.

Bateman, A and Fonagy, P (2009) Randomized Control Trial of Outpatient Mentalization-based Treatment Versus Structured Clinical Management for Borderline Personality Disorder. *American Journal of Psychiatry*, 166(12): 1355–64.

Battle, C L, Shea, M T, Johnson, D M, Yen, S, Zlotnick, C, Zanarini, M C and Morey, L C (2004) Childhood Maltreatment Associated with Adult Personality Disorders: Findings from the Collaborative Longitudinal Personality Disorders Study. *Journal of Personality Disorders*, 18: 193–211.

Beales, D (2001) Continuing Stigmatisation by Psychiatrists. *British Journal of Psychiatry*, 178: 475.

Beck, U (1992) *Risk Society: Towards a New Modernity.* Munich: Sage.

Becker, H (2008) *Outsiders.* London: Simon and Schuster.

Berenbaum, H, Thompson, R, Milandek, M, Boden, M and Bredemeier, K (2008) Psychological Trauma and Schizotypal Personality Disorder. *Journal of Abnormal Psychology*, 117: 502–19.

Beresford, P (2002) Thinking about 'Mental Health': Towards a Social Model. *Journal of Mental Health*, 11(6): 581–84.

Beresford, P (2005) Social Approaches to Madness and Distress: User Perspectives and User Knowledges, in Tew, J (ed) *Social Perspectives in Mental Health: Developing Social Models to Understand and Work with Mental Distress* (pp 32–53). London: Jessica Kingsley.

Beresford, P (2012) What Service Users Want from Social Workers. *Community Care.* [online] Available at: www.communitycare.co.uk/2012/04/27/what-service-users-want-from-social-workers/ (accessed 7 May 2016).

Beresford, P and Branfield, F (2006) Developing Inclusive Partnerships: User-Defined Outcomes, Networking and Knowledge – A Case Study. *Health & Social Care in the Community*, 14(5): 436–44.

Beresford, P and Croft, S (2001) Service Users' Knowledges and the Social Construction of Social Work. *Journal of Social Work*, 1(3): 295–316.

Beresford, P and Croft, S (2004) Service Users and Practitioners Reunited: The Key Component for Social Work Reform. *British Journal of Social Work*, 34: 53–68.

Berg, E B, Barry, J and Chandler, J P (2008) New Public Management and Social Work in Sweden and England: Challenges and Opportunities for Staff in Predominantly Female Organizations. *International Journal of Sociology and Social Policy*, 28(3/4) 114–28.

Bernstein, D, Iscan, C and Maser, J (2007) Opinions of Personality Disorder Experts Regarding the DSM-IV Personality Disorder Classification System. *Journal of Personality Disorders*, 21: 536–51.

Bhugra, D (2008) Renewing Psychiatry's Contract with Society. *Psychiatric Bulleting*, 32: 281–3.

Biegel, D, Pernice-Duca, F, Chang, C, Chung, C, Oh Min, M and D'Angelo, L (2013) Family Social Networks and Recovery from Severe Mental Illness of Clubhouse Members. *Journal of Family Social Work*, 16(4): 274–96.

Bisman, C (2004) Social Work Values: The Moral Core of the Profession. *British Journal of Social Work*, 34(1): 109–23.

Blackburn, R (1988) On Moral Judgements and Personality Disorders. *British Journal of Psychiatry*, 153: 505–12.

Bland, A and Rossen, E (2005) Clinical Supervision of Nurses Working with Patients with Borderline Personality Disorder. *Issues in Mental Health Nursing*, 26: 507–17.

Blitz, L, Pender Greene, M, Bernabei, S and Shah, V (2014) Think Creatively and Act Decisively: Creating an Antiracist Alliance of Social Workers. *Social Work* 59(4): 347–50.

Blom-Cooper, L (1996) Some Reflections on Public Inquiries, in Peay, J (ed) *Inquiries after Homicide.* London: Duckworth.

Borman, E (2011) Changing Professionalism, in Bhugra, D, Malik, A and Ikkos, G (eds) *Psychiatry's Contract with Society: Concepts, Controversies and Consequences* (pp 209–21). Oxford: Oxford University Press.

Bortoli, L and Dolan, M (2015) Decision Making in Social Work with Families and Children: Developing Decision Aids Compatible with Cognition. *British Journal of Social Work*, 45(7): 2142–60.

Bovaird, T (2007) Beyond Engagement and Participation: User and Community Coproduction of Public Services. *Public Administration Review*, 67(5): 846–60.

Bowers, L (2002) *Dangerous and Severe Personality Disorder: Response and Role of the Psychiatric Team.* London: Routledge.

Bowers, A (2011) Clinical Risk Assessment and Management of Service Users. *Clinical Governance*, 16(3): 190–200.

Bowlby, J (1973) *Attachment and Loss: Separation, Anxiety and Anger*. Michigan: Basic Books.

Boyle, K (2016) What Are the Consequences for Human Rights If We Change Our Relationship with the EU? [online] Available at: http://ukandeu.ac.uk/explainers/what-are-the-consequences-for-human-rights-if-we-change-our-relationship-with-the-eu/ (accessed 8 August 2016).

Bracken, P and Thomas, P (2004) Post-psychiatry: A New Direction for Mental Health. *British Medical Journal*, 322: 724–27.

Bracken, P and Thomas, P (2005) *Post-psychiatry: Mental Health in a Postmodern World*. Oxford: Oxford University Press.

Breckenridge, J and James, K (2010) Educating Social Work Students in Mutifaceted Interventions for Trauma. *Social Work Education*, 29(3): 259–75.

Briere, J and Hodges, M (2010) Assessing the Effects of Early and Later Childhood Trauma in Adults, in Vermetter, E, Lanius, R and Palin, C (eds) *The Impact of Early Life Trauma on Health and Disease*. Cambridge, UK: Cambridge University Press.

British Association of Social Workers (BASW) (2012) The Code of Ethics for Social Work. [online] Available at: www.basw.co.uk/resource/?id=501 (accessed 15 October 2012).

British Association of Social Workers (2013) *BASW*. BASW/IFSW Policy on Effective and Ethical Working Environments for Social Work: The Responsibilities of Employers of Social Workers. [online] Available at: http://cdn.basw.co.uk/upload/basw_124655-10.pdf (accessed 2 August 2016).

British Association of Social Workers (2015a) *BASW*. BASW Human Rights Policy. [online] Available at: http://cdn.basw.co.uk/upload/basw_30635-1.pdf (accessed 8 August 2016).

British Association of Social Workers (2015b) *BASW*. Professional Capabilities Framework. *BASW*. [online] Available at: www.basw.co.uk/pcf (accessed 9 January 2016).

British Broadcasting Company (2015) Mental Health Services Budget Cut by 8%. *BBC*. [online] Available at: www.bbc.co.uk/news/health-31970871 (accessed 9 April 2016).

Breeze, J A and Repper, J (1998) Struggling for Control: The Care Experiences of "Difficult" Patients in Mental Health Services, *Journal of Advanced Nursing*, 28(6): 1301–1311.

Breslau, N, Wilcox, H, Storr, C, Lucia, V and Antony, C (2004) Trauma Exposure and Posttraumatic Stress Disorder: A Study of Youths in Urban America. *Journal of Urban Health*, 81(4): 530–44.

Broadhurst, K, Wastell, D, White, S, Hall, C, Peckover, S, Thompson, K, Pithouse, A and Davey, D (2010) Performing Initial Assessment: Identifying the Latent Conditions for Error at the Front Door of Local Authority Children's Services. *British Journal of Social Work*, 40(2): 352–70.

Bruch, C (2002) The New 'Public': The Globalization of Public Participation. Washington: Environmental Law Institute.

Brudney, J and England, R (1983) Toward a Definition of the Coproduction Concept. *Public Administration Review*, 43(1): 59–65.

Brown, K, and Young, N (2008) Building Capacity for Service User and Carer Involvement. *Social Work Education*, 27: 84–96.

Buckley, H, Carr, N and Whelan, S (2011) Like Walking on Eggshells: Service User Views and Expectations of the Child Protection System. *Child and Family Social Work*, 16(1): 101–10.

Burton, A (1990) Personality Disorder: The Limits to Intervention. *Practice*, 4(4): 221–8.

Bussey, M and Wise, J (2007) *Trauma Transformed*. New York: Columbia University Press.

Butler, J (1998) Merely Cultural. *New Left Review*, 227: 33–44.

Campbell, J and Davidson, G (2012) *Post-qualifying Mental Health Social Work Practice*. London: Sage.

Campbell, J, Brophy, L, Healy, B and O'Brien, M (2006) International Perspectives on the Use of Community Treatment Orders: Implications for Mental Health Social Workers. *British Journal of Social Workers*, 36: 1101–18.

Carey, M (2007) White Collar Proletariat? Braverman, the Deskilling/Upskilling of Social Work and the Life of the Agency Care Manager. *Journal of Social Work* 7(1): 93–114.

Carr, D (1991) *Educating the Virtues: An Essay on the Philosophical Psychology of Moral Development and Education*. London: Routledge.

Carter, R (2015) Implementing the Employer Standards Tells Our Social Workers We Respect Them. *Community Care*. [online] Available at: www.communitycare.co.uk/2015/03/18/implementing-employer-standards-tells-social-workers-respect/ (accessed 11 August 2016).

Castillo, H (2003) *Personality Disorder: Temperament or Trauma?* London: Jessica Kingsley.

Castillo, H (2010) The Process of Recovery for People Diagnosed with Personality Disorder: A Case Study of the Haven. Unpublished doctoral dissertation, Anglia Ruskin University, Cambridge.

Castillo, H (2011) Evaluation of KUF Awareness Module. [online] Available at: www.thehavenproject.org.uk/Training/KUFEvaluationEastOfEnglandOct2011.pdf (accessed 7 May 2016).

Castillo, H, Allen, L and Coxhead, N (2001) The Hurtfulness of a Diagnosis: User Research about PD. *Mental Health Practice*, 4(9): 16–19.

Celinski, M (2012) Challenge-Resilience-Resourcefulness as the Essential Components of Recovery, in Gow, K and Celinski, M (eds) *Individual Trauma: Recovering from Deep Wounds and Exploring the Potential for Renewal*. New York: Nova Science Publishing.

Charmaz, K (2008) Grounded Theory in the 21st Century: Applications for Advancing Social Justice Studies. In Denzin, N K and Lincoln, Y S (eds) *Strategies of Qualitative Inquiry* (pp 203–41). Thousand Oaks, CA: Sage.

Cherry, S (2005) *Transforming Behaviour: Pro-Social Modelling in Practice*. Cullompton: Willan.

Cherry, S (2010) *Transforming Behaviour: Pro-Social Modelling in Practice* (2nd edn). Cullompton: Willan.

Clark, C (2006) Moral Character in Social Work. *British Journal of Social Work*, 36(1): 75–89.

Clark, C (2007) Professional Responsibility, Misconduct and Practical Reason. *Ethics and Social Welfare*, 1(1): 56–75.

Clark, L (2009) Stability and Change in Personality Disorder. *Current Directions in Psychological Science*, 18(1): 27–31.

Clarke, J and Newman, J (1993) The Right to Manage: A Second Managerial Revolution? *Cultural Studies*, 7(3): 427–41.

Cleary, M, Siegfried, M and Walter, G (2002) Experience, Knowledge and Attitudes of Mental Health Staff Regarding Clients with a Borderline Personality Disorder. *International Journal of Mental Health Nursing*, 11(3): 186–91.

Cleckley, H (1982) *The Mask of Sanity*. St Louis: New American Library.

Coffey, M, Dugdill, L and Tattersall, A (2004) Stress in Social Services: Mental Wellbeing, Constraints and Job Satisfaction. *British Journal of Social Work*, 34(5): 735–46.

Coid, J, Yang, M, Tyrer, P, Roberts, A and Ullrich, S (2006) Prevalence and Correlates of Personality Disorder. *British Journal of Psychiatry*, 188(5): 423–31.

Collins, S and Long, A (2003) Working with the Psychological Effects of Trauma: Consequences for Mental Health-Care Workers – A Literature Review. *Journal of Psychiatric and Mental Health Nursing*, 10: 417–24.

Corbett, K and Westwood, T (2005). 'Dangerous and Severe Personality Disorder': Manifestation of the Risk Society. *Critical Public Health*, 15(2): 121–33.

Council of Europe (1953) *European Convention of Human Rights*. [online] Available at: www.echr.coe.int/Documents/Convention_ENG.pdf (accessed 16 March 2016).

Crisp, C and McCave, E (2007) Gay Affirmative Practice: A Model for Social Work Practice with Gay, Lesbian and Bisexual Youth. *Child Adolescent Social Work Journal*, 24: 403–21.

Currier, G and Briere, J (2000) Trauma Orientation and Detection of Violence Histories in the Psychiatric Emergency Service. *The Journal of Nervous and Mental Disease*, 188(9): 622–4.

Dalgard, O (2008) Social Inequalities in Mental Health in Norway: Possible Explanatory Factors. *International Journal for Equity in Health*, 7(1): 27. DOI: 10.1186/1475-9276-7-27.

Davies, K, Gray, M and Webb, S (2014) Putting the Parity into Service-User Participation: An Integrated Model of Social Justice. *International Journal of Social Welfare*, 23: 119–27.

D'Cruz, H and Jones, M (2004) *Social Work Research: Ethical and Political Contexts*. London: Sage.

Deegan, P E (2001) Recovery as a Self-directed Process of Healing and Transformation. Occupational Therapy in Mental Health. *A Journal of Psychosocial Practice & Research*, 17(3/4): 5–21.

Deepak, A C, Rountree, M A and Scott, J (2015) Delivering Diversity and Social Justice in Social Work Educations: The Power of Context. *Journal of Progressive Human Services*, 26: 107–25.

Denscombe, M (2003) *The Good Research Guide for Small Scale Social Research Projects*. Berkshire: Open University Press.

Dent, M and Barry, J (2004) New Public Management and the Profession in the UK: Reconfiguring Control, in Dent, M, Chandler, J and Barry, J (eds) *Questioning the New Public Management*. Aldershot: Ashgate Publishing Limited.

Denzin, N K and Lincoln, Y S (2000) Introduction: The Discipline and Practice of Qualitative Research, in Denzin, N K and Lincoln, Y S (eds) *The Handbook of Qualitative Research* (2nd ed). Thousand Oaks, CA: Sage.

Denzin, N K and Lincoln, Y S (2008) *The Landscape of Qualitative Research* (3rd edn). Thousand Oaks, CA: Sage.

Derrida, J (2002) *Writing and Difference* in Bass, A (trans). London: Routledge.

Dimaggio, G and Norcross, J C (2008) Treating Patients with Two or More Personality Disorders: An Introduction. *Journal of Clinical Psychology*, 64(2): 127–38.

Diver, C (2008) Enhancing Social Work Management: Theory and Best Practice from the UK and USA. *Journal of Inter-professional Care*, 22(2): 221.

Downie, R (2011) Professions, Related Occupations, and Ethics, in Bhugra, D, Malik, A and Ikkos, G (eds) *Psychiatry's Contract with Society: Concepts, Controversies and Consequences* (pp 23–35). Oxford: Oxford University Press.

Duggan, C, Husband, N, Smailagic, N, Ferriter, N and Adams, C (2007) The Use of Pharmacological Treatments for People with Personality Disorder: A Systematic Review of Randomised Control Trials. *Journal of Personality & Mental Health*, 1(2): 95–125.

Duggan, M (2002) *Modernising the Social Model in Mental Health: A Discussion Paper*. Leeds: Training Organisation for the Personal Social Services.

Durkheim, E (2013) *The Division of Labour in Society*. London: Palgrave.

Dustin, D (2007) *McDonaldization of Social Work*. London: Routledge.

Eisenberg, N, Spinard, T and Sadovsky, A (2005) Empathy Related Responding in Children, in Killen, M and Smetna, J G (eds) *Handbook of Moral Development*. (pp 517–49). Mahwah, NJ: Lawrence Erlbaum.

Eldergill, A (2002) Is Anyone Safe? Civil Compulsion Under the Draft Mental Health Bill. *Journal of Mental Health Law*, 5: 331–59.

Ellis, K (2014) Professional Discretion and Adult Social Work: Exploring Its Nature and Scope on the Front Line of Personalisation. *The British Journal of Social Work*, 44(8): 2272–89.

Ellul, J (1964) *The Technological Society*. Toronto: Vintage.

Erikson, E H (1968) *Identity, Youth & Crisis*. New York: W. W. Norton.

Estroff, S (1989) Self, Identify and Subjective Experiences of Schizophrenia: In Search of the Subject. *Schizophrenia Bulletin*, 15(2): 189–96.

Eur-Lex (2016) *Charter of Fundamental Rights*. [online] Available at: http://eur-lex.europa.eu/legal-content/EN/TXT/?uri=LEGISSUM:l33501 (accessed 16 March 2016).

European Institute (2016) The Implications of Brexit for Fundamental Rights Protection in the UK. [online] Available at: www.lse.ac.uk/europeanInstitute/LSE-Commission/Hearing-6--The-implications-of-Brexit-for-fundamental-rights-protection-in-the-UK.pdf (accessed 8 August 2016).

Evans, T (2011) Professionals Managers and Discretion: Critiquing Street Level Bureaucracy. *British Journal of Social Work*, 41(2): 368–86.

Fallon, P (2003) Travelling through the System: The Lived Experience of People with Borderline Personality Disorder in Contact with Psychiatric Services. *Journal of Psychiatric and Mental Health Nursing*, 10: 393–400.

Fawcett, B and Featherstone, B (1999) Setting the Scene, in Fawcett, B, Featherstone, B, Fook, J and Rossiter, A (eds) *Practice and Research in Social Work: Postmodern Feminist Perspectives* (pp 5–24). London: Routledge.

Feinstein, A R (1972) XIII. On Homogeneity, Taxonomy, and Nosography. *Clinical Pharmacology & Therapeutics*, 13(1): 114–29.

Ferguson, I and Lavalette, M (2004) Beyond Power Discourse: Alienation and Social Work. *British Journal of Social Work*, 34(3): 297–312.

Feurino, L and Silk, K (2011) State of the Art in the Pharmacologic Treatment of Borderline Personality Disorder. *Current Psychiatric Reports*, 13(1): 69–75.

Figley, C R (ed) (1995) *Compassion Fatigue: Coping with Secondary Traumatic Stress Disorder in Those Who Treat the Traumatized*. New York: Brunner/Mazel.

Finlay, L (2002) 'Outing' the Researcher: The Provenance, Process and Practice of Reflexivity. *Qualitative Health Research*, 12(3): 531–45.

Forrester, D, Holland, S, Williams, A and Copello, A (2016) Helping Families Where Parents Misuse Drugs or Alcohol? A Mixed Methods Comparative Evaluation of an Intensive Family Preservation Service. *Child & Family Social Work*, 21(1): 65–75.

Forrester, D, Kershaw, S, Moss, H and Hughes, L (2008) Communication Skills in Child Protection: How Do Social Workers Talk to Parents? *Child & Family Social Work*, 13: 41–51.

Foucault, M (1997) *Ethics, Subjectivity and Truth*. New York: New Press.

Fox, J (2008) The Importance of Expertise by Experience in Mental Health Services. *International Journal of Leadership in Public Services*, 4(4): 39–43.

Frances, A (2012) How Many Billions a Year Will the DSM-V Cost? *Bloomberg*. [online] Available at: www.bloomberg.com/news/2012-12-20/how-many-billions-a-year-will-the-dsm-5-cost-.html (accessed 15 February 2013).

Fraser, N (1998) Social Justice in the Age of Identity Politics: Redistribution, Recognition, Participation. [online] Availableat:www.ssoar.info/ssoar/bitstream/handle/document/12624/ssoar-1998-fraser-social_justice_in_the_age.pdf?sequence=1 (accessed 31 July 2016).

Fraser, N (2005) Reframing Justice in a Globalising World. *New Left Review*, 36: 69–88.

Freire, P (1970) *Pedagogy of the Oppressed*. New York: Herder & Herder.

Frisby, D (1992) *The Alienated Mind: The Sociology of Knowledge in Germany, 1918–1933*. London: Routledge.

Garret, P (2005) Social Work's 'Electronic Turn': Notes on the Deployment of Information and Communication Technologies in Social Work with Children and Families. *Critical Social Policy*, 25(4): 529–53.

Geertz, C (1977) *The Interpretation of Cultures*. New York: Basic Books.

Gergen, K and Gergen, M (2003) *Social Construction: A Reader*. Thousand Oaks, CA: Sage.

Giddens, A (1999) *The Third Way: The Renewal of Social Democracy*. Chichester: John Wiley.

Giddens, A (2013) *Essentials of Sociology*. London: Norton.

Giddens, A and Sutton, P (2013) *Sociology*. Cambridge: Polity.

Giffin, J (2008) Family Experience of Borderline Personality Disorder. *Australian & New Zealand Journal of Family Therapy*, 29(3): 133–38.

Glaser, B and Strauss, A (1967) *The Discovery of Grounded Theory: Strategies for Qualitative Research*. New York: Aldine de Guyter.

Glaser, B (2002) Constructivist Grounded Theory? *Forum: Qualitative Social Research*, 3(3) Art. 12.

Glicken, M D (2004) *Using the Strengths Perspective in Social Work Practice*. Boston: Pearson Education.

Goffman, E (1990) *The Presentation of Self in Everyday Life*. London: Penguin.

Gow, K (2012) Overview: Conceptualising Trauma as a Deep Wound While Continuing to Live One's Life, in Gow, K and Celinski, M (eds) *Individual Trauma; Recovering from Deep Wounds and Exploring the Potential for Renewal*. New York: Nova Science Publishing.

Gow, K and Celinski, M (2012) *Individual Trauma; Recovering from Deep Wounds and Exploring the Potential for Renewal*. New York: Nova Science Publishing.

Gray, M and Webb, S (2009) *Social Work Theories and Methods*. [online] Available at: http://s3.amazonaws.com/academia.edu.documents/30555938/FrontSocialWorkTheoriesandMethods2013.pdf?AWSAccessKeyId=AKIAIWOWYYGZ2Y53UL3A&Expires=1490299661&Signature=tJmyaOcy8EA3LUxp%2BWyxN7TfQJE%3D&response-content-disposition=inline%3B%20filename%3DSocial_Work_Theories_and_Methods_-_2nd_E.pdf (accessed 16 March 2016).

Graybar, S and Boutilier, L (2002) Nontraumatic Pathways to Borderline Personality Disorder. *Psychotherapy, Theory, Research, Practice and Training*, 39: 152–62.

Gregor, C and Smith, H (2009) 'I'm Not a Performing Monkey'. Reflections on the Emotional Experience of Developing a Collaborative Training Initiative between Service Users and Lecturer. *Journal of Social Work Practice*, 23(1): 21–34.

Grinker, R, Werble, B and Drye, R (1968) *The Borderline Syndrome*. New York: Basic Books.

Guardian, The (2013) Carers Should Be Monitored for Mental Health Problems, Warn Doctors. *The Guardian*. [online] Available at: www.theguardian.com/society/2013/may/11/carers-monitored-mental-health-problems (accessed 23 April 2016).

Guba, E G and Lincoln, Y S (1989) *Fourth Generation Evaluation*. Newbury Park, CA: Sage.

Gunderson, J (2009) Borderline Personality Disorder: Ontogeny of a Diagnosis. *American Journal of Psychiatry*, 166: 530–9.

Gunnell, D, Donovan, J, Barnes, M, Davies, R, Hawton, K, Kapur, N, Hollingworth, W and Metcalfe, C (2015) The 2008 Global Financial Crisis: Effects on Mental Health and Suicide. [online] Available at: www.bris.ac.uk/media-library/sites/policybristol/documents/PolicyReport-3-Suicide-recession.pdf (accessed 8 August 2016).

Habermas, J (1990) *Moral Consciousness and Communicative Action*. Cambridge: Polity Press.

Haggerty, K and Ericson, R (2000) The Surveillant Assemblage. *British Journal of Sociology*, 51(4): 605–22.

Hanisch, C (1970) The Personal Is Political, in Firestone, S and Koedt, A (eds) *Notes from the Second Year* (pp 76–8). New York: Radical Feminism.

Hare, R D (2003) Psychopathy and Risk for Recidivism and Violence, in Gray, N, Laing, J and Noaks, L (eds) *Criminal Justice, Mental Health and the Politics of Risk* (pp 27–49). London: Cavendish.

Hartman, A (1990) Many Ways of Knowing. *Social Work*, 35(1): 3–4.

Haslam, N (2005) Dimensions of Folk Psychiatry. *Review of General Psychology*, 9: 35–47.

Haslam, N and Whelan, J (2008) Human Natures: Psychological Essentialism in Thinking about Differences between People. *Social and Personality Psychology Compass*, 2/3: 1297–312.

Haslam, N, Bastian, B, Bain, P and Kashima, Y (2006) Psychological Essentialism, Implicit Theories, and Intergroup Relations. *Group Processes and Intergroup Relations*, 9: 63–76.

Hayles, N (1999) *How We Became Posthuman: Virtual Bodies in Cybernetics, Literature, and Informatics*. Chicago: University of Chicago Press.

Head, S, Baker, J and Williamson, D (1991) Family Environment Characteristics and Dependent Personality Disorder. *Journal of Personality Disorders*, 5: 256–63.

Health and Care Professions Council (HCPC) (2012) Standards of Proficiency. HCPC. [online] Available at: www.hcpc-uk.org.uk/assets/documents/10003B08Standardsofproficiency-SocialworkersinEngland.pdf (accessed 9 March 2017).

Health & Safety Executive (HSE) (2010) *Management Standards*. [online] Available at www.hse.gov.uk/stress/standards/ (accessed 4 April 2016).

Healy, L (2008) Exploring the History of Social Work as a Human Rights Profession. *International Social Work*, 51(6): 735–48.

Hebebrand, J and Buitelaar, J K (2011) On the Way to DSM-V. *European Child and Adolescent Psychiatry*, 20(2): 57–60.

Heffernan, K (2006) Social Work, New Public Management and the Language of 'Service User'. *British Journal of Social Work*, 36(1): 139–47.

Hegel, G (1977) *The Phenomenology of the Spirit*. Oxford: Oxford University Press.

Herman, J L (1992) *Trauma and Recovery: The Aftermath of Violence – From Domestic Abuse to Political Terror*. New York: Basic Books.

Hersch, R (2008) Confronting Myths and Stereotypes about Borderline Personality Disorder. *Social Work in Mental Health*, 6(12): 13–32.

Hinshelwood, R (1999) The Difficult Patient. *British Journal of Psychiatry*, 174: 187–90.

Hodder, L and Gow, K (2012) The Long-Term Effects of Childhood Sexual Abuse, in Gow, K and Celinski, M (eds) *Individual Trauma* (pp 101–13). New York: Nova Science Publishers.

Hodge, D (2014) Affirming Diversity, Difference and the Basic Human Rights of Those with Whom We Disagree: A Difficult Task but Worth the Challenge – A Reply to Bolen and Dessel. *Journal of Social Work Education*, 50: 153–63. DOI: 10.1080/10437797.2014.856240.

Hoffman, M (2001) Toward a Comprehensive Empathy-based Theory of Prosocial Moral Development, in Bohart, A and Stipeck, D (eds) *Constructive and Destructive Behaviour: Implications for Family, School and Society* (pp 61–86). Washington DC: American Psychological Association.

Holscher, D and Bozalek, G (2012) Encountering the Other across the Divides: Re-rounding Social Justice as a Guiding Principle for Social Work with Refugees and Other Vulnerable Groups. *British Journal of Social Work*, 42: 1093–112. DOI: 10.1093/bjsw/bcs061.

Holstein, J A and Gubrium, J F (2004) The Active Interview, in Silverman, D (ed) *Qualitative Research: Theory, Method and Practice* (pp 140–62). London: Sage.

Honneth, A (1997) A Society Without Humiliation. *European Journal of Philosophy*, 5(3): 306–24.

Hood, C (1991) A Public Management for All Seasons. *Public Administration*, 69: 3–19.

Horlick-Jones, T (2005) On 'Risk Work': Professional Discourse, Accountability and Everyday Action. *Health Risk and Society*, 7(3): 293–308.

Horn, N, Johnstone, L and Brooke, S (2007) Some Service User Perspectives on the Diagnosis of Borderline Personality Disorder. *Journal of Mental Health*, 16: 255–69.

Horovitz, A V (2002) *Creating Mental Illness*. Chicago: Chicago University Press.

Horton, A and Lekka, P (2012) Borderline Personality Disorder: Pharmacotherapy and Psychological Interventions in Inpatient Services after the Introduction of NICE Guidelines in the UK. *European Psychiatry*, 27(Supp/1): 926.

House of Commons Constitution Committee (2008) *European Union (Amendment) Bill and the Lisbon Treaty: Implications for the UK Constitution*. [online] Available at: www.publications.parliament.uk/pa/ld200708/ldselect/ldconst/84/84.pdf (accessed 16 March 2016).

Houston, S (2009) Communication, Recognition and Social Work: Aligning the Ethical Theories of Habermas and Honneth. *British Journal of Social Work*, 39: 1274–90.

Houston, S, Skehill, C, Pinkerton, J and Campbell, J (2005) Prying Open the Space for Social Work in the New Millennium: Four Theoretical Perspectives on Transformative Practice. *Social Work and Social Sciences Review*, 12(1): 35–52.

Howell, A J, Weikum, B A and Dyck, H L (2011) Psychological Essentialism and Its Association with Stigmatization. *Personality and Individual Differences*, 50(1): 95–100.

Huang, Y, Kotov, R, Girolamo, G, Preti, A, Angermeyer, M, Benjet, C et al. (2009) DSM IV Personality Disorders in WHO World Mental Health Surveys. *British Journal of Psychiatry*, 195(1): 46–53.

Huxley, P, Evans, S, Gately, C, Webber, M, Mears, A, Palak, S, Kendall, T, Medina, J and Katona, C (2005) Stress and Pressures in Mental Health Social Work: The Worker Speaks. *British Journal Social Work*, 35(7): 1063–79.

Ikkos, G, McQueen, D and St John-Smith, P (2011) Psychiatry's Contract with Society: What Is Expected? *Acta Psychiatrica Scandanavica*, 124: 1–3.

Ingleby, D (1981) *Critical Psychiatry: The Politics of Mental Health*. Harmondsworth: Penguin.

Institute for Fiscal Studies (2010) Spending Review 2010. [online] Available at: www.ifs.org.uk/projects/346 (accessed 15 October 2012).

International Federation of Social Workers (IFSW) (1988) 'Human Rights', in International Policy Papers. Geneva: IFSW.

International Federation of Social Workers (IFSW) (2014) Global Definition of Social Work. [online] Available at: http://ifsworg/get-involved/global-definition-of-social-work/ (accessed 13 March 2016).

INVOLVE (2006) Involving Marginalised and Vulnerable People in Research: A Consultation Document. [online] Available at: www.invo.org.uk/pdfs/Involving%20Marginalised%20and%20VullGroups%20in%20Researchver2.pdf (accessed 23 January 2006).

Irvine, A (1996) The Social Work Role with Personality Disordered Clients, in Fuller, R and Petch, A (eds) *Practitioner Research: The Reflexive Social Worker* (pp 124–37). Buckingham: Open University Press.

Irvine, J, Molyneux, J and Gillman, M (2014) Providing a Link with the Real World: Learning from the Student Experience of Service User and Carer Involvement. *Social Work Education*, 34(2): 138–50.

Jablensky, A (2005) Categories, Dimensions & Prototypes: Critical Issues or Psychiatric Classification. *Psychopathology*, 38(4): 201–5.

Jablensky, A and Kendell, R E (2002) Criteria for Assessing a Classification in Psychiatry, in Maj, M, Gaebel, W, Lopez-Ibor, J and Sartorius, N. (eds) *Psychiatric Diagnosis and Classification* (pp 1–25). New York: John Wiley & Sons.

Jaspers, K (1963) *General Psychopathology* (7th ed). (Translated Hoenig, J and Hamilton, M W). Manchester: Manchester University Press.

Jones, R, Van den Bree, M, Ferriter, M and Taylor, P (2010) Childhood Risk Factors for Offending before First Psychiatric Admission for People with Schizophrenia: A Case-Control Study of High Security Hospital Admissions. *Behavioral Sciences & the Law*, 28(3): 351–65.

Jordan, B (1975) Is the Client a Fellow Citizen? *Social Work Today*, 30 October.

Jordon, B (2001) Tough Love: Social Work, Social Exclusion and the Third Way. *British Journal or Social Work*, 31(4), 527–46.

Kairys, S and Johnson, C (2002) Committee on Child Abuse and Neglect: The Psychological Maltreatment of Children - Technical Report. *Paediatrics*, 109(4): 1–3.

Kemshall, H (2010) Risk Rationalities in Contemporary Social Work Policy and Practice. *The British Journal of Social Work*, 40(4): 1247–62.

Kernberg, O (1967) Borderline Personality Organization. *Journal of the American Psychoanalytical Association*, 15: 641–85.

Keys, D and Lambert, G (2002) Concept of 'Personality Disorder' and Its Relationship to Social Work. *Australian Social Work*, 55(3): 161–8.

Khan, M R (1963) The Concept of Cumulative Trauma. *Psychoanalytic Study of the Child*, 18: 286–306.

King, D W, Leskin, G A, King, L A and Weathers, F W (1998) Confirmatory Factor Analysis of the Clinicial-Administered PTSD Scale: Evidence for the Dimensionality of Post-traumatic Stress Disorder. *Psychological Assessment*, 10: 90–6.

Kinman, G and Grant, L (2011) Exploring Stress Resilience in Trainee Social Workers: The Role of Emotional and Social Competencies. *British Journal of Social Work*, 41(2): 261–75.

Kirmayer, L (2005) Culture, Context and Experience in Psychiatric Diagnosis. *Pyschopathology*, 38(4): 192–96.

Kirmayer, L, Lemelson, R and Barad, M (2007) Understanding Trauma: Integrating Biological, Clinical and Cultural Perspectives. New York: Cambridge University Press.

Klein, M (1959) Our Adult World and Its Roots in Infancy. *Human Relations*, 12: 291–303.

Kleinman, A (1999) Experience and its Moral Modes: Culture, Human Conditions, and Disorder. In Peterson, G B (ed), *The Tanner Lectures on Human Values, Vol 20* (pp 357–420). Salt Lake City, UT: University of Utah Press.

Knight, C (2015) Trauma Informed Social Work Practice: Practice Considerations and Challenges. *Clinical Social Work Journal*, 43(1): 25–37.

Knight, R (1953) Borderline States. *Bulletin of the Menninger Clinic*, 17(1): 1–12.

Koekkoek, B, van Meijel, B and Hutschemaekers, G (2006) 'Difficult Patients' in Mental Health Care: A Review. *Psychiatric Services*, 57(6): 795–802.

Kris, E (1956) The Recovery of Childhood Memories in Psychoanalysis. *Psychoanalytical Study of the Child*, 11: 54–88.

Kvale, S (1996) *Interviews: An Introduction to Qualitative Research Interviewing*. Thousand Oaks, CA: Sage.

Kvaternik, I and Grebenc, V (2009) The Role of Social Work in the Field of Mental Health: Dual Diagnoses as a Challenge for Social Workers. *European Journal of Social Work*, 12(4): 509–21.

Lamont, S and Brunero, S (2009) Personality Disorder Prevalence and Treatment Outcomes: A Literature Review. *Issues in Mental Health Nursing*, 30: 631–7.

Langan, J and Lindow, V (2004) *Mental Health Service User Involvement in Risk Assessment and Management*. Bristol: Policy Press.

Lanius, R, Vermetten, E and Pain, C (2010) The Impact of Early Life Trauma on Health and Disease: The Hidden Epidemic. Cambridge: Cambridge University Press.

Latalova, K, Ociskova, M, Prasko, J, Sedlackova, Z and Kamaradova, D (2015) If You Label Me, Go with Your Therapy Somewhere! Borderline Personality Disorder and Stigma. *European Psychiatry*, 30 (Supp/1): 1520.

Laulik, S, Chou, S, Browne, K D and Allam, J (2013) The Link between Personality Disorder and Parenting Behaviors: A Systematic Review. *Aggression and Violent Behavior*, 18(6): 644–55.

Lee, R M (1993) *Doing Research on Sensitive Topics*. London: Sage.

Lee, R M (2006) Childhood Trauma and Personality Disorder: Toward a Biological Model. *Current Psychiatry Reports*, 8(1): 43–52.

Lefebvre, R, Howe, N and Guile, J (2004) Perceptions of Mother-Child Relationships in Families of Children with Borderline Traits. *Perspectives on Psychological Science*, 43: 345–53.

Lester, H and Glasby, J (2006) *Mental Health Policy and Practice.* Hampshire: Palgrave.

Lewis, G and Appleby, L (1988) Personality Disorder: The Patients Psychiatrists Dislike. *British Journal of Psychiatry*, 153: 44–9.

Leyens, J, Rodriguez-Perez, A, Rodriguez-Torres, R, Gaunt, R, Paladino, M P, Rodriguez-Torres, R, Gaunt, R, Paladino, M-P, Vaes, J and Demoulin, S (2001) Psychological Essentialism and the Differential Attribution of Uniquely Human Emotions to in Groups and Outgroups. *European Journal Social Psychology*, 31: 395–411.

Lishman, J (2009) *Communication in Social Work*. Hampshire: Palgrave.

Lister, R (1998) From Equality to Social Inclusion: New Labour and the Welfare State. *Critical Social Policy*, 18(2): 215–25.

Lister, R (1998) Citizen in Action: Citizenship and Community Development in Northern Ireland Context. *Community Development Journal*, 33(3): 226–35.

Lister, R (2007) Citizenship on the Margins: Citizenship, Social Work and Social Action. *European Journal of Social Work*, 1(1): 5–18.

Livesley, W J (1998) Suggestions for a Framework for an Empirically Based Classification of Personality Disorder. *Canadian Journal of Psychiatry*, 43: 137–47.

Livesley, W J (2003) *The Practical Management of Personality Disorder*. New York: Guildford Press.

Livesley, W J (2010) Confusion and Incoherence in the Classification of Personality Disorder: Commentary on the Preliminary Proposals for DSM-5. *Psychological Injury and Law*, 3: 304–13.

Livesley, W J (2011) An Empirically-Based Classification of Personality Disorder. *Journal of Personality Disorders*, 25(3): 398–420.

Livesley, W J, Schroeder, M L, Jackson, D N and Jang, K L (1994) Categorical Distinctions in the Study of Personality Disorder: Implications for Classification. *Journal of Abnormal Psychology*, 103: 6–17.

Local Government Association (LGA) (2014) *Social Worker Standards: The Standards for the Employers of Social Workers in England*. [online] Available at www.local.gov.uk/workforce/-/journal_content/56/10180/3511605/ARTICLE (accessed 4 April 2016).

Longley, D (1996) *Health Care Constitutions.* London: Cavendish Publishing.

Lubit, R, Rovine, D, DeFrancisci, L and Eth, S (2003) Impact of Trauma on Children. *Journal of Psychiatric Practice*, 9(2): 128–38.

Luborsky, L (1984) *Principles of Psychoanalytic Psychotherapy: A Manual for Supportive-Expressive Treatment*. New York: Basic Books.

Lundy, C (2011) *Social Work, Social Justice and Human Rights: A Structural Approach to Practice*. Ontario: University of Toronto Press

Malik, K (1996) *The Meaning of Race: Race, History and Culture in Western Society*. New York: New York University Press.

Malik, M and Hussein, N (2009) Qualitative Outcome for Community Treatment Orders. *The Psychiatrist*, 33: 437–8.

Mangan, C, Miller, R and Ward, C (2015) Knowing Me, Knowing You: Inter-professional Working between General Practice and Social Care. *Journal of Integrated Care*, 23(2): 62–73.

Manthorpe, J, Moriaty, J, Hussein, S, Stevens, M and Sharpe, E (2015) Content and Purpose of Supervision in Social Work Practice in England: Views of Newly Qualified Social Workers, Managers and Directors. *British Journal of Social Work*, 45: 52–68.

Markham, D (2003) Attitudes towards Patients with a Diagnosis of Borderline Personality Disorder: Social Rejection and Dangerousness. *Journal of Mental Health*, 12(6): 595–612.

Marlowe, J M and Adamson, C E (2011) Teaching Trauma: Critically Engaging a Troublesome Term. *Social Work Education: Special Issue: Health and Wellbeing*, 30(6): 623–34.

Marshall, T H (1987) *Citizenship and Social Class* London: Pluto.

Massie, H and Szajnberg, N (2008) *Lives across Time/Growing Up: Paths to Emotional Health and Emotional Illness from Birth to 30 in 76 People*. London: Karnac.

Mattheys, K (2015) The Coalition, Austerity and Mental Health. *Disability & Society*, 30(3): 475–8.

McBeath, G and Webb, S (2002) Virtue Ethics and Social Work: Being Lucky, Realistic and Not Doing One's Duty. *British Journal of Social Work*, 32: 1015–36.

McCann, L and Pearlman, L (1990) Vicarious Traumatization: A Framework for Understanding the Psychological Effects of Working with Victims. *Journal of Traumatic Stress*, 3(1): 131–49.

McCrae, R and Costa, P (2003) Personality in Adulthood: A Five-Factor Theory Perspective (2nd ed). New York: Guilford.

McKim, L and Smith-Adcock, S (2013) Trauma Counsellors' Quality of Life. *International Journal for the Advancement of Counselling*, 36(1): 58–69.

McLeod, E, Bywaters, P, Tanner, D and Hirsch, M (2008) For the Sake of Their Health: Older Service Users' Requirements for Social Care to Facilitate Access to Social Networks Following Hospital Discharge. *British Journal of Social Work*, 38: 73–90. DOI: 10.1093/bjsw/bcl341.

McMain, S, Links, P, Guimond, T, Wnuk, S, Eynan, R, Bergmans, Y and Warwar, S (2013) An Exploratory Study of the Relationship between Changes in Emotion and Cognitive Processes and Treatment Outcome in Borderline Personality Disorder. *Psychotherapy Research*, 23(6): 658–73.

McNee, L, Donoghue, C and Coppola, A (2014) A Team Approach to Borderline Personality Disorder. *Mental Health Practice*, 17(10): 33–5.

Mead, G H (1962) *Mind, Self and Society from the Standpoint of a Social Behaviourist*. Chicago: University of Chicago Press.

Miller, C and Stirling, S (2004) *Coproduction in Children's Services*. London: Office for Public Management.

Miller, S G (1994) Borderline Personality Disorder from the Patient's Perspective. *Psychiatry*, 45(2): 1215–19.

Mills, C (1970) *The Sociological Imagination*. Harmondsworth: Penguin.

Mills, J, Bonner, A and Francis, K (2006) Adopting a Constructivist Approach to Grounded Theory: Implications for Research Design. *International Journal of Nursing Practice*, 12(1): 8–16.

Monahan, J and Steadman, H J (1983) Crime and Mental Disorder: An Epidemiological Approach. *Crime and Justice*, 4: 145–89.

Munro, E (2004) The Impact of Audit on Social Work Practice. *British Journal of Social Work*, 34(8): 1075–95.

Munroe, J F, Shay, J, Fisher, L, Makary, C, Rapperport, K and Zimering, R (1995) Preventing Compassion Fatigue: A Treatment Team Model, in Figley, R (ed) *Compassion Fatigue: Coping with Secondary Traumatic Stress Disorder in Those Who Treat the Traumatized* (pp 209–31). New York: Brunner/Mazel.

Munroe, E and Hubbard, A (2011) A Systems Approach to Evaluating Organisational Change in Children's Social Care. *British Journal of Social Work*, 41(4): 726–43.

Murphy, D, Duggan, M and Joseph, S (2013) Relationship Based Social Work and Its Compatibility with the Person-Centred Approach: Principled versus Instrumental Perspectives. *British Journal of Social Work*, 43: 703–19.

Nash, M (2006) *Public Protection and the Criminal Justice Process*. Oxford: Oxford University Press.

Nathan, J and Webber, M (2010) Mental Health Social Work and the Bureau-Medicalisation of Mental Health Care: Identity in a Changing World. *Journal of Social Work Practice*, 24(1): 15–28.

National Institute for Clinical Excellence (2009) Borderline Personality Disorder: Treatment & Management. [online] Available at: www.nice.org.uk/guidance/CG78 (accessed 15 July 2014).

National Institute for Mental Health (NIMHE) (2003) *Personality Disorder: No Longer a Diagnosis of Exclusion*. Barbican, London.

Needham, C (2007) Realising the Potential of Co-production: Negotiating Improvements in Public Services. *Social Policy & Society*, 7(2): 221–31.

Nehls, N (1998) Borderline Personality Disorder: Gender Stereotypes, Stigma and Limited Systems of Care. *Issues in Mental Health Nursing*, 19: 97–112.

Nehls, N (1999) Borderline Personality Disorder: The Voice of Patients. *Research in Nursing and Health*, 22: 285–93.

Nelson, D, Price, E and Zubrzycki, J (2013) Integrating Human Rights and Trauma Frameworks in Social Work with People from Refugee Backgrounds. *Australian Social Work*, 67(4): 567–81.

Newhill, C E and Korr, W S (2004) Practice with People with Severe Mental Illness: Rewards, Challenges, Burdens. *Health & Social Work*, 29(4): 297–305.

Newton-Howes, G, Tyrer, P, Anagnostakis, K, Cooper, S, Bowden-Jones, O and Weaver, T (2010) The Prevalence of Personality Disorder, Its Comorbidity with Mental State Disorders and Its Clinical Significance in Community Mental Health Teams. *Social Psychiatry & Psychiatric Epidemiology*, 45(4): 453–60.

Norton, K (2012) Boundaries and Borderline Personality Disorder, in Kelly, G and Aiyegbusi, A (eds) *Professional and Therapeutic Boundaries in Forensic Mental Health Practice*. London: Jessica Kingsley.

Nussbaum, M and Sen, A (1993) *The Quality of Life*. Oxford: Oxford University Press.

Nussbaum, M (2006) *Frontiers of Justice: Disability, Nationality and Species Membership*. Cambridge, MA: Harvard University Press.

O' Brien, A and Calderwood, K (2010) Living in the Shadows: A Canadian Experience of Mental Health Social Work. *Social Work in Mental Health*, 8: 319–35.

O'Leary, P, Tsui, M-S and Ruch, G (2013) The Boundaries of the Social Work Relationship Revisited: Towards a Connected, Inclusive and Dynamic Conceptualization. *British Journal of Social Work*, 43(1): 135–53.

O'Malley, P (2008) Experiments in Risk and Criminal Justice. *Theoretical Criminology*, 12(4): 451–69.

Olsson, I and Dahl, A (2012) Avoidant Personality Problems – Their Association with Somatic and Mental Health, Lifestyle, and Social Network. A Community-Based Study. *Comprehensive Psychiatry*, 53(6): 813–21.

Ostrom, E (1996) Crossing the Great Divide: Coproduction, Synergy and Development. *World Development*, 24(6): 1073–87.

Pahl, R (1990) Prophets, Ethnographers and Social Glue: Civil Society and Social Order. Paper given at ESRC/CNRS Workshop on Citizenship, Social Order and Civilising Processes, Cumberland Lodge, September 1990.

Paris, J (1996) *Social Factors in the Personality Disorders: A Biopsychosocial Approach to Etiology and Treatment*. New York: Cambridge University Press.

Paris, J (1998) Does Childhood Trauma Cause Personality Disorders in Adults? *Canadian Journal of Psychiatry*, 43: 148–53.

Paris, J (2008) *Treatment of Borderline Personality Disorder: A Guide to Evidence-Based Practice*. New York: Guildford.

Parker, I, Georgaca, E, Harper, D, McLaughlin, T and Stowell-Smith, M (1995) *Deconstructing Psychopathology*. London: Sage.

Parton, N (2008) Changes in the Form of Knowledge in Social Work: From the Social to the Informational. *British Journal of Social Work*, 38: 253–69.

Patterson, G, DeBaryshe, B and Ramsey, E (1989) A developmental Perspective on Antisocial Behaviour. *American Psychologist*, 44: 329–35.

Pemberton, M (2012) Healthy Competition in the NHS is a Sick Joke. *Telegraph*. [online] Available at: www.telegraph.co.uk/news/features/9193015/healthy-competition-in-the-NHS-is-a-sick-joke.html (accessed 13 October 2012).

Perez-Sola, V (2011) Treatment Resistance in Borderline Personality Disorder. *European Psychiatry*, 26(Supp/1): 2024.

Philip, M (1979). Notes on the Form of Knowledge in Social Work. *Sociological Review*, 27(1): 83–111.

Pidd, F and Feigenbaum, J (2007) Personality Disorder: Still Everybody's Business? *Mental Health Review Journal*, 12(4): 5–12.

Pilgrim, D (2001) Disordered Personalities and Disordered Concepts. *Journal of Mental Health*, 10(3): 253–65.

Pilgrim, D and Rogers, A (2003) Mental Disorder and Violence: An Empirical Picture in Context. *Journal of Mental Health*, 12(1): 7–18.

Pilknonis, P A, Hallquist, M N, Morse, J Q and Stepp, S D (2011) Striking the (Im)proper Balance between Scientific Advances and Clinical Utility: Commentary on the DSM-5 Proposal for Personality Disorder. *Personality Disorders Theory, Research and Treatment*, 2(1): 68–82.

Pinel, P (1801) *A Treatise on Insanity* (Translated by Davis, D, 1806). New York: Hafner.

Pines, A (1993) Burnout, in Goldberger, L and Breznitz, S (eds) *Handbook of Stress* (2nd edn) (pp 386–403). New York: The Free Press.

Plumb, S (2005) The Social/Trauma Model: Mapping the Mental Health Consequences of Childhood Sexual Abuse and Similar Experiences, in Tew, J (ed) *Social Perspectives in Mental Health* (pp 112–28). London: Jessica Kingsley.

Pollock, R (2014) *The Public Service Transformation Network*. London: Public Services Executive.

Postle, K and Beresford, P (2007) Capacity Building and the Reception of Political Participation: A Role for Social Care Workers. *British Journal of Social Work*, 37(1): 143–58.

Prichard, J C (1837) *A Treatise on Insanity and Other Disorders Affecting the Mind*. London: Sherwood, Gilbert & Piper.

Rameriz, R (1999) Value Co-production: Intellectual Origins and Implications for Practice and Research. *Strategic Management Journal*, 20(1): 49–65.

Ramon, S (1985) *Psychiatry in Britain*. Beckenham: Croom Helm.

Ramon, S (2005) Approaches to Risk in Mental Health: A Multidisciplinary Discourse, in J Tew (ed) *Social Perspectives in Mental Health: Developing Social Models to Understand and Work with Mental Distress* (pp 184–200). London: Jessica Kingsley Publishers.

Ramon, S, Castillo, H and Morant, N (2001) Experiencing Personality Disorder: A Participative Research. *International Journal of Social Psychiatry*, 47(4): 1–15.

Rawls, J (1971) *A Theory of Justice*. Cambridge, MA: Harvard University Press.

Read, J, Goodman, L, Morrison, A and Ross, C (2004) Childhood Trauma, Psychosis and Schizophrenia: A Literature Review with Theoretical and Clinical Implications. *Acta Psychiatrica Scandinavia*, 112: 330–50.

Read, J, Haslem, N, Sayce, L and Davies, E (2006) Prejudice and Schizophrenia: A Review of the 'Mental Illness Is an Illness Like Any Other' Approach. *Acta Psychiatrica Scandinava*, 114(5): 303–18. DOI: 10.1111/j.1600-0447.2006.00824.x

Reamer, F (2005) *Ethical and Legal Standards in Social Work*. [online] Available at: http://digitalcommons.ric.edu/cgi/viewcontent.cgi?article=1176&context=facultypublications (accessed 15 March 2016).

Reich, D and Zanarini, M (2001) Developmental Aspects of Borderline Personality Disorder. *Harvard Review of Psychiatry*, 9(6): 294–301.

Reimer, M (2010) Moral Aspects of Psychiatric Diagnosis: The Cluster B Personality Disorders. *Neuroethics*, 3(2): 173–84.

Reisch, M and Jani, J (2012) The New Politics of Social Work Practice: Understanding Context to Promote Change. *British Journal of Social Work*, 42: 1132–50.

Rendu, A, Moran, P, Patel, A, Knapp, M and Mann, A (2002) Economic Impact of Personality Disorders in Primary Care Attenders. *British Journal of Psychiatry*, 181: 62–6.

Renouf, N and Bland, R (2005) Navigating Stormy Waters: Challenges and Opportunities for Social Work in Mental Health. *Australian Social Work*, 58(4): 419–30.

Repper, J and Breeze, J (2007) User and Carer Involvement in the Training and Education of Health Professionals: A Review of the Literature. *International Journal of Nursing Studies*, 44(3): 511–19.

Ro, E, Stringer, D and Clark, L (2012) The Schedule for Nonadaptive and Adaptive Personality: A Useful Tool for Diagnosis and Classification of Personality Disorder, in Widiger, T (ed) *The Oxford Handbook of Personality Disorders* (pp 58–82). Oxford: Oxford University Press.

Rogosch, F and Cicchetti, D (2005) Child Maltreatment, Attention Networks, and Potential Precursors to Borderline Personality Disorder. *Development & Psychopathology*, 17: 1071–89. DOI: 10.1017/s0954579405050509

Rohleder, P (2007) HIV and the 'Other'. *Psychodynamic Practice: Individuals, Groups and Organisations*, 13(4): 401–12.

Rose, N (1986) The Discipline of Mental Health, in Miller, P and Rose, N (eds) *The Power of Psychiatry* (pp 43–85). Cambridge: Polity.

Rose, N (1996) The Death of the Social? Refiguring the Territory of Government. *Economy and Society*, 25(3): 327–56.

Rose, N (2000) Government and Control. *British Journal of Criminology*, 40: 321–39.

Rossiter, R and Black, J (2009) Challenging Therapeutic Pessimism: Borderline Personality Disorder and Co-morbid Substance Misuse. *Mental Health and Substance Use Dual Diagnosis*, 2(2): 140–53.

Rothbart, M and Taylor, M (1992) Category Labels and Social Reality: Do We View Social Categories as Natural Kinds? in Semin, G R and Fielder, K (eds) *Language and Social Cognition* (pp 11–36). London: Sage.

Rovinelli-Heller, N and Gittan, A (2011) *Mental Health & Social Problems: A Social Work Perspective*. New York: Routledge.

Rozenberg, J (2001) Law Chief in Call to Lock Up Child Sex Suspects. *Telegraph*. [online] Available at: www.telegraph.co.uk/news/uknews/1366393/Law-chief-in-call-to-lock-up-child-sex-suspects.html (accessed 13 October 2012).

Rubin, H and Rubin, I (1995) *Qualitative Interviewing: The Art of Hearing Data*. Thousand Oaks, CA: Sage.

Ruch, G (2012) Where Have All the Feelings Gone? Developing Reflective and Relationship Based Management in Child-care Social Work. *British Journal of Social Work*, 42(7): 1315–32.

Rutter, M (1987) Temperament, Personality and Personality Disorder. *British Journal of Psychiatry*, 150: 443–58.

Ryan, M, Dowden, C, Healy, B and Renouf, N (2005) Watching the Experts: Findings from an Australian Study of Expertise in Mental Health Social Work. *Journal of Social Work*, 5(30): 279–98.

Ryan, P and Morgan, S (2004) Assertive Outreach: A Strengths Approach to Policy and Practice. London: Elsevier.

Ryan, P, Ramon, S and Greacen, T (2012) *Empowerment, Lifelong Learning and Recovery in Mental Health*. Basingstoke: Palgrave Macmillan

Saleeby, D (1997) *The Strengths Perspective in Social Work Practice*. Longman: Michigan.

Sampson, E (2003) Possessive Individualism and the Self-contained Ideal, in Gergen, M and Gergen, K (eds) *Social Construction: A Reader* (pp 123–9). Thousand Oaks, CA: Sage.

Samuel, D and Widiger, T (2008) Clinicians' Judgements of Clinical Utility: A Comparison of DSM IV and Five Factor Models. *Journal of Abnormal Psychology*, 115: 298–308.

Sanislow, C and McGlashan, T (1998) Treatment Outcome of Personality Disorders. *Canadian Journal of Psychiatry*, 43: 237–50.

Schakleton, R (1972) The Greatest Happiness of the Greatest Number: The History of Bentham's Phrase. Banbury: Voltaire Foundation.

Schneider, K (1958) *Psychopathic Personalities*. London: Cassell.

Schraer, R (2015) Most Authorities Don't Know Whether Social Workers' Caseloads Are at an Unsafe Level. *Community Care*. [online] Available at: www.communitycare.co.uk/2015/03/11/most-authorities-unaware-of-whether-social-workers-caseloads-are-at-an-unsafe-level (accessed 11 August 2016).

Schon, D (1983) *The Reflective Practitioner: How Professionals Think in Action*. New York: Basic Books.

Scott, A (2000) Risk Society or Angst Society? Two Views of Risk, Consciousness and Community, in Van Loon, J (ed) *The Risk Society and Beyond – Critical Issues for Social Theory* (pp 33–46). London: Sage.

Scourfield, J, Roen, K and McDermott, L (2008) Lesbian, Gay, Bisexual and Transgender Young People's Experience of Distress: Resilience, Ambivalence and Self-destructive Behaviour. *Health and Social Care in the Community*, 16(3): 329–36.

Segal, E (2012) Beyond the Pale of Psychoanalysis: Relational Theory and Generalist Social Work Practice. *Clinical Social Work Journal*, 41(4): 376–86.

Segal, J (1992) *Melanie Klein*. London: Sage.

Sen, A (2009) *The Idea of Justice*. Cambridge, MA: Harvard University Press.

Shah, N (2016) David Cameron Has Created a Mental Health Crisis that Can't Be Solved with £1 Billion Worth of Funding. *The Independent*. [online] Available at: www.independent.co.uk/voices/david-cameron-has-created-a-mental-health-crisis-that-cant-be-solved-with-1-billion-worth-of-funding-a6807631.html (accessed 8 August 2016).

Simon, B (2007) Respect, Equality and Power: A Social Psychological Perspective. *Gruppendynamik und Organisationberatung*, 38(3): 309–26.

Simon, W (2012) *Mourning the Person One Could Have Become: On the Road from Trauma to Authenticity*. Plymouth: Aronson.

Social Care Institute for Excellence (SCIE) (2008) SCIE Research Briefing 26: Mental Health and Social Work. *SCIE*. [online] Available at: www.scie.org.uk/publications/briefings/briefing26/ (accessed 27 February 2015).

Social Care Institute for Excellent (SCIE) (2013) *Co-production in Social Care: What It Is and How to Do It*. London: SCIE.

Social Research Association (2003) Ethical Guidelines. [online] Available at: www.the-sra.org.uk/guidelines.htm (accessed 16 March 2006).

Solas, J (2008) Social Work and Social Justice: What Are We Fighting For? *Australian Social Work*, 61(2): 124–36.

Soteman, D, Hakkaart-van-Roijen, L, Verheul, R and Busschbach, J (2008) The Economic Burden of Personality Disorders in Mental Health Care. *Journal of Clinical Psychiatry*, 69(2): 259–65.

Sroufe, L, Egeland, B, Carlson, E and Collins, W (2005) *The Development of the Person: The Minnesota Study of Risk and Adaptation from Birth to Adulthood*. New York: Guildford Press.

Stalker, K, Ferguson, I and Barclay, A (2005) 'It Is a Horrible Term for Someone': Service User and Provider Perspectives on 'Personality Disorder'. *Disability & Society*, 20(4): 359–73.

Stamm, B H (ed) (1999) Secondary Traumatic Stress: Self-care Issues for Clinicians, Researchers, and Educators (2nd ed). Lutherville, MD: Sidran.

Stanford, S (2010) Speaking Back to Fear: Responding to the Moral Dilemmas of Risk in Social Work Practice. *British Journal of Social Work*, 40(4): 1065–80.

Starmer, K (2016) The Conservatives Need to Accept the Human Rights Act, and Move On. *The Guardian*. [online] Available at: www.theguardian.com/commentisfree/2016/may/18/conservatives-human-rights-act (accessed 8 August 2016).

Stern, A (1938) Psychoanalytic Investigation and Therapy in the Borderline Group of Neurosis. *The Psychoanalytic Quarterly*, 7: 467–89.

Stern, D T (2004) *Measuring Medical Professionalism*. Oxford: Oxford University Press.

Stoffers, J, Vollm, B, Rucker, G, Timmer, A and Lieb, K (2009) A Meta-Analysis of Randomized Control Trials. *European Psychiatry*, 24 (Supp/1): 1086.

Stuart, G, Moore, T, Gordon, K, Ramsey, S and Kahler, C (2006) Psychopathology in Women Arrested for Domestic Violence. *Journal of Interpersonal Violence*, 21: 376–89.

Szajnberg, N, Goldenberg, A and Harau, U (2010) Early Trauma, Later Outcome: Results from Longitudinal Studies and Clinical Observations, in Lanius, R, Vermetten, E and Pain, C (eds) *The Impact of Early Life Trauma on Health and Disease: The Hidden Epidemic* (pp 33–43). Cambridge: Cambridge University Press.

Taylor-Gooby, P (2011) Root and Branch Restructuring to Achieve Major Cuts: The Social Policy Programme of the 2010 UK Coalition Government. *Social Policy and Administration*,46(1): 61–82.

Tetley, A, Jinks, M, Howells, K, Dugan, C, McMurran, M, Huband, N, Geelan, S, Milton, J and Kaul, A (2012) A Preliminary Investigation of Services for People with Personality Disorder in the East Midlands Region of England. *Personality & Mental Health*, 6(1): 33–44.

Tew, J (2002) Going Social: Championing a Holistic Model of Mental Distress within Professional Education. *Social Work Education*, 21(2): 143–55.

Tew, J (2005) *Social Perspectives in Mental Health: Developing Social Models to Understand and Work with Mental Distress*. London: Jessica Kingsley.

Tew, J (2006) Understanding Power and Powerlessness: Towards a Framework for Emancipatory Practice. *Journal of Social Work*, 6(1): 33–51.

Tew, J, Ramon, S, Slade, M, Bird, V, Melton, J and Le Boutillier, C (2012) Social Factors and Recovery from Mental Health Difficulties: A Review of the Evidence. *British Journal of Social Work*, 42: 443–60.

The College of Social Work (2012) *The Professional Capabilities Framework*. [online] Available at: www.tcsw.org.uk/pcf.aspx (accessed 31 August 2013).

Titus, N (2004) *Personality Disorder: Challenges for Social Work*. Social Work Mongraphs: University of East Anglia.

Touraine, A (1995) *Critique of Modernity*. Oxford: Blackwell.

Tritter, J and McCallum, A (2006) The Snakes and Ladders of User Involvement: Moving beyond Arnstein. *Health Policy*, 76(2): 156–68.

Trotter, C (2004) *Helping Abused Children and Their Families*. Crows Nest, NSW: Sage.

Trull, T (2005) Dimensional Models of Personality Disorder: Coverage and Cutoffs. *Journal of Personality Disorders*, 19(3): 262–82.

Turner, K, Lovell, K and Brooker, A (2011) '... And They All Liv'd Happily Ever After' 'Recovery' or Discovery of the Self in Personality Disorder? *Psychodynamic Practice*, 17(3): 341–6.

Tyrer, P (2000) *Personality Disorders: Diagnosis, Management and Course*. Oxford: Butterworth Heinemann.

United Kingdom, Department of Health (1983) *Mental Health Act*. Amended 2007. London: HMSO.

United Kingdom, Department of Health (1990) *National Health Service & Community Care Act*. London: HMSO.

United Kingdom, Department of Health and Home Office (1992) *Review of Health and Social Services for Mentally Disordered Offenders and Others Requiring Similar Services. Final Summary Report.* Cm 2088. London.

United Kingdom, Department of Health (1998) *Modernising Social Services.* London: HMSO.

United Kingdom, Department of Health (1999a) *Managing Dangerous People with Severe Personality Disorder: Proposals for Policy Development.* London: HMSO.

United Kingdom, Department of Health (1999b) *Reform of the Mental Health Act 1983: Proposals for Consultation.* London: The Stationary Office.

United Kingdom, Department of Health (1999c) National Service Framework: Mental Health. [online] Available at: www.gov.uk/government/publications/quality-standards-for-mental-health-services (accessed 16 April 2015).

United Kingdom, Department of Health (2005a) *Personality Disorder Capacity Plans.* London: HMSO.

United Kingdom, Department of Health (2005b) *Creating a Patient-Led NHS: Delivering the NHS Improvement Plan.* London: HMSO.

United Kingdom, Department of Health (2005c) *Research Governance Framework.* [online] Available at: www.gov.uk/govevrnment/uploads/system/uploads/attachment_data/file/139565/dh)4122427.pdf (accessed 22 January 2016).

United Kingdom, Department of Health (2006) *National Health Services Act.* London: HMSO.

United Kingdom, Department of Health and Ministry of Justice (2007) *The Knowledge and Understanding Framework.* [online] Available at www.personalitydisorderkuf.org.uk (accessed 14 May 2012).

United Kingdom, Department of Health (2008) *Modernising Mental Health Services: Safe, Sound and Supportive.* London: HMSO.

United Kingdom, Department of Health (2009) *New Horizons: A Shared Vision for Mental Health.* London: HMSO.

United Kingdom, Department of Health (2010) *No Health Without Mental Health: A Cross-Government Mental Health Outcomes Strategy for People of all Ages.* London: HMSO.

United Kingdom, Department of Health (2014) *The Care Act.* London: HMSO.

United Kingdom. Department of Health (2015a) *Knowledge and Skills Statements for Social Workers in Adult Services.* London: HMSO.

United Kingdom, Department of Health (2015b) *No Voice Unheard, No Right Ignored.* London: HMSO.

United Nations (1948) The Universal Declaration of Human Rights. [online] Available at: www.ohchr.org/EN/UDHR/Documents/UDHR_Translations/eng.pdf (accessed 3 August 2016).

Van der Kolk, B (1997) Post-traumatic Stress Disorder and Memory. *The Psychiatric Times*, 14(3): 1–5.

Wade, D T and Halligan, P W (2004) Do Biomedical Models of Illness Make for Good Healthcare Systems? *British Medical Journal*, 329: 1398–401.

Watts, D and Morgan, G (1994) Malignant Alienation: Dangers for Patients Who Are Hard to Like. *British Journal of Psychiatry*, 164: 11–15.

Webb, S A (2001) Some Considerations on the Validity of Evidence-Based Practice in Social Work. *British Journal of Social Work*, 31: 51–79.

Webb, S A (2006) *Social Work in a Risk Society: Social and Political Perspectives.* London: Palgrave Macmillan.

Weber, M (2012) *The Theory of Social and Economic Organization.* Eastford, CT: Martino Fine Books.

Weinberg, D (2007) Habermas, Rights and the Learning Disabled Citizen. *Social Theory and Health*, 5: 70–87.

Weisner, M and Silbereisen, R K (2003) Trajectories of Delinquent Behaviour in Adolescence and Their Covariates: Relations with Initial and Time-averaged Factors. *Journal of Adolescence*, 26: 753–71.

Wendland, J, Brisson, J, Medeiros, M, Camon-Senechal, L, Aidane, E, David, M, Serres, J, Cohen, D and Rabain, D (2014) Mothers with Borderline Personality Disorder: Transition to Parenthood, Parent-Infant Interaction, and Preventative/Therapeutic Approach. *Clinical Psychology: Science & Practice*, 21(2): 139–53.

Westberg, J and Jason, H (2001) *Fostering Reflection and Providing Feedback: Helping Others Learn from Experience.* New York: Springer.

Wheeler, M (2016) Cavalier with Our Constitution: A Charter Too Far. [online] Available at: https://ukhumanrightsblog.com/2016/02/09/cavalier-with-our-constitution-a-charter-too-far/ (accessed 8 August 2016).

Widiger, T, and Costa, P (2002) Five-Factor Model Personality Disorder Research, in Costa, Jr. P T and Widiger, T A (eds) *Personality Disorders and the Five-Factor Model of Personality* (2nd ed) (pp 59–87). Washington, DC: American Psychological Association.

Widiger, T and Lowe, J (2008) A Dimensional Model of Personality Disorder: Proposal for DSM V. *Psychiatric Clinics of North America*, 31: 363–78.

Wilson, J P (2006) *The Posttraumatic Self: Restoring Meaning and Wholeness to Personality*. New York: Routledge.

Wilson, G and Daly, M (2007) Shaping the Future of Mental Health Policy and Legislation in Northern Ireland: The Impact of Service User and Professional Social Work Discourses. *British Journal of Social Work*, 37: 423–39.

Wilson, K, Ruch, G, Lymbery, M and Cooper, A (2011) Social Work: An Introduction to Contemporary Practice. Harlow: Pearson.

Winnicott, D W (1957) On the Capacity to be Alone. *International Journal of Psychoanalysis*, 39(5): 416–20.

Winnicott, D W (1973) *The Child, the Family, and the Outside World*. Middlesex: Penguin.

Winship, G and Hardy, S (2007) Perspectives on the Prevalence and Treatment of Personality Disorder. *Journal of Psychiatric and Mental Health Nursing*, 14(2): 148–54.

Wirth, W (1991) Responding to Citizens' Needs: From Bureaucratic Accountability to Individual Coproduction in the Public Sector, in Kaufmann, F X (ed) *The Public Sector: Challenge for Coordination and Learning* (pp 69–85). New York/ Berlin: Walter de Gruyter.

Wittchen, H, Knappe, S and Schumann, G (2014) The Psychological Perspective on Mental Health and Mental Disorder Research: Introduction to the ROAMER Work Package 5 Consensus Document. *International Journal of Methods in Psychiatric Research*, 23(s1), 15–27.

Wood, T E, Englander-Golden, P, Golden, D E and Pillai, V K (2010) Improving Addictions Treatment Outcomes by Empowering Self and Others. *International Journal of Mental Health Nursing*, 19(5): 363–8.

World Health Organisation (WHO) (1992) *Tenth Revision of the International Classification of Diseases and Related Health Problems*. Geneva: World Health Organisation.

World Health Organisation (WHO) (2012) *Schizophrenia*. [online] Available at: www.who.int/mental_health/management/schizophrenia/en/ (accessed 22 October 2012).

Wright, K, Haigh, K and McKeown, M (2007) Reclaiming the Humanity in Personality Disorder. *International Journal of Mental Health Nursing*, 16: 236–46.

Yasqur, B S (2012) *Monthly Prescribing Reference*. Controversial DSM-5 Changes: Task Force Chair Addresses Critical Questions. [online] Available at: www.empr.com/controversial-dsm-5-changes-task-force-chair-addresses-critical-questions/article/273675/2/ (accessed 15 February 2012).

Yen, S, Shea, M T, Battle, C L, Johnson, D M, Zlotnick, C, Dolan-Sewell, R, Skodol, A E, Grilo, C M, Gunderson, J G, Sanislow, C A, Zanarini, M C, Bender, D S, Rettew, J B and McGlashan, T H (2002) Traumatic Exposure and Posttraumatic Stress Disorder in Borderline, Schizotypal, Avoidant, and Obsessive-Compulsive Personality Disorders: Findings from the Collaborative Longitudinal Personality Disorders Study. *Journal of Nervous and Mental Diseases*, 190: 510–18.

Young, I (1990) *Justice and the Politics of Difference*. Princeton: Princeton University Press.

Young, J (1999) *The Exclusive Society*. London: Sage.

Yzerbyt, V, Corneille, O and Esrrada, C (2001) The Interplay of Subjective Essentialism and Entitativity in the Formation of Stereotypes. *Personality & Social Psychology Review*, 5(2): 141–55.

Yzerbyt, V, Rocher, S and Schadron, G (1997) Stereotypes as Explanations: A Subjective Essentialistic View of Group Perception, in Spears, R, Oakes, P J, Ellemers, N and Haslam, S A (eds) *The Social Psychology of Stereotyping and Group Life* (pp 20–50). Cambridge: Blackwell.

Zanarini, M (2000) Childhood Experiences Associated with the Development of Borderline Personality Disorder. *Psychiatric Clinics of North America*, 23: 89–101.

Zanarini, M, Frances, R, Frankenburg, F, Dubo, E, Sickel, A, Trikha, A, Levin, A and Reynolds, V (1998) Comorbidity of Borderline Personality Disorder. *American Journal of Psychiatry*, 155: 1733–39.

Zanarini, M, Yong, L and Frankenburg, F (2002) Severity of Reported Sexual Abuse and Its Relationship to Severity of Borderline Psychopathology and Psychosocial Impairment among Borderline Inpatients. *Journal of Nervous & Mental Diseases*, 190: 381–7.

Zimmerman, M and Coryell, W (1989) DSM III Personality Disorder Diagnoses in a Non-patient Sample: Demographic Correlates and Comorbidity. *Archives of General Psychiatry*, 46: 682–9.

Index